HUMAN GROUND, SPIRITUAL GROUND

D1496112

# Human Ground
## Spiritual Ground

## Paradise Lost and Found

**A REFLECTION ON CENTERING PRAYER'S CONCEPTUAL BACKGROUND**

## Kess Frey

[PORTAL BOOKS]

2012
PORTAL BOOKS
An imprint of Anthroposophic Press/SteinerBooks
610 Main St., Great Barrington, MA
www.steinerbooks.org

Cover and book design: William Jens Jensen
Cover image: *The Temptation of Eve* (1808), William Blake; watercolor for John Milton's *Paradise Lost*, book IX (1604):

*"So saying, her rash hand in evil hour*
*Forth reaching to the Fruit, she pluck'd, she eat."*

LIBRARY OF CONGRESS CATALOGING-IN-PUBLICATION DATA
Frey, Kessler.
  Human ground, spiritual ground : paradise lost and found : a reflection on centering prayer's conceptual background / Kess Frey.
      p. cm.
  Includes bibliographical references.
  ISBN 978-0-9831984-5-1 — ISBN 978-0-9831984-8-2 (ebook)
  1. Psychology and religion. 2. Psychology, Religious. 3. Keating, Thomas. 4. Contemplation. I. Title.
    BL53.F74 2012
    200.1'9—dc23
                                                    2012026599

# Contents

*This book is gratefully dedicated to*
*Thomas Keating, William A. Meninger, and Basil Pennington,*
*the spiritual fathers and founders of*
*Centering Prayer in our time.*

# ACKNOWLEDGMENTS

The outer world is filled with a wide variety of people, images, organizations, and influences. Blessed are those that lead us toward the discovery and awakening of our true self and life in spiritual ground (our life in Christ). I have many people to thank, beginning with my late parents of loving memory, Charles and Lorraine Frey, and my beloved uncle, Dr. Andy Adams, who introduced me to philosophy and psychology at a time when I needed to find direction in life. I'm also grateful to my sister, Diane Frey, and to numerous personal friends and teachers—academic, secular, and spiritual—who've guided and inspired me.

This book would not have been possible without the excellent teaching, writing and example of Fr. Thomas Keating, the kind and humble monk I first met in June of 1989 at Saint Benedict's Monastery in Snowmass, Colorado. It's my hope that this book may help others toward a deeper study and appreciation of Thomas Keating's works. The training I've received through Contemplative Outreach, the spiritual network founded by Thomas Keating and others, together with what I've received from some of Contemplative Outreach's wonderful staff over the years are invaluable to me.

I am particularly grateful to several past and present inmates of the Anchorage Correctional Complex, East and West, who have participated in religious services and a small Centering Prayer Group with me; they are a challenging, down-to-earth audience, with whom I've tried out and developed some of the core ideas in this book.

I am especially grateful to Fr. Carl Arico for his openness to my writing, his help, support, and encouragement, and for the kind, generous foreword he has written; to Gene Gollogly and Martin Rowe for believing in this book; and to Jens Jensen for book design, etc.

Lastly, experiencing my false self, I've often felt inadequate and continue to realize I can do nothing worthwhile in this work without the inner inspiration, blessing, and help of the Spirit and the gift of Centering Prayer.

*Kess Frey*
*February 8, 2012*

# FOREWORD

Iam excited that my fellow contemplative pilgrim, Kess Frey, is having his book published by Portal Books. Our relationship goes back quite a few years. I know him as a committed seeker and a faithful Centering Prayer practitioner. I have watched him grow on many levels of his being, especially in his spirituality. We always make time for one another at many of the conferences, retreats, and workshops sponsored by Contemplative Outreach. He is an avid reader and student of spirituality in general. Kess has shared many of his manuscripts with me and has a gift of asking the hard questions and looking for the deeper meaning of life, taking the insights of his own experience and rooting them in his Christian beliefs. I have shared some of his manuscripts with my friends, and his writings have always sparked serious and prayerful discussion. I am sure it will also be so with this book.

Here, in *Human Ground, Spiritual Ground,* we celebrate the mystery of the incarnation—the word of God infleshed in our human experience and in God's likeness. One of Kess's mentors is the Trappist, Fr. Thomas Keating. Thomas is a founding member of Contemplative Outreach, an organism created to promote the Christian Contemplative Tradition through Centering Prayer. In the course of his teachings, Thomas has developed a conceptual background for the prayer and has often spoken about the next generation that will tap into his teaching and take it to the next level. Kess has done this; he has that ability and shows it in this work. It makes the spiritual journey one that is attainable to many, because it is life lived to the fullest on God's terms with Jesus showing us the way.

Just look at the table of contents and you will see what I mean. The information shared here will help the reader see life's journey through new eyes. Pondering this material, one begins to learn how to celebrate the events of each day more deeply. By seeing God's hands at work in our reactions to the experiences of each day, our hearts are touched—and not just touched, but also, like being in love, perhaps our daily life may be turned upside down, especially as we come to see the journey as a spirituality of diminishment rather than one of achievement: "He must increase; I must decrease" (John 3:30).

This wisdom is rooted in the experience of Jesus, as recorded in Matthew 4:1 to 11—the temptation event. Here the tempter knew that if he could find in Jesus the least bit of attachment to security and survival (change these stones into bread), affection and esteem (throw yourself down, the angels will take care of you), power and control (I will give you all these kingdoms if you worship me), he would have an opening to manipulate Jesus and influence his ministry and doing the will of His Father. Each of us knows this is also our struggle—to feel secure, to be well regarded, and to be always in control. These needs in themselves are part of the human condition. But when we hold on to them disproportionately, when we hold on to them as the keys to our happiness and fulfillment, we stagnate our journey.

How to deal with these all-too-common tensions? An answer is spelled out in these reflections as Kess explores the Conceptual Background of Centering Prayer. Centering Prayer is not only a prayer practice, but also a key to life. Why? It celebrates the depth of one's consent to the Divine presence and action in daily life. What does that mean?

It is a way of life worth exploring. Read this book as if you were dining at an exquisite banquet—ever so gently. This book is definitely not for speed-reading. It is meant to be read thoughtfully and gradually, its contents to be digested slowly. In so doing, you will discover why Kess Frey's book is called "Human Ground, Spiritual Ground."

*Fr. Carl J. Arico*
*A founding member of Contemplative Outreach*
*Author of* A Taste of Silence

# PREFACE

The idea for this book began at Contemplative Outreach's 2004 Annual Meeting in Toronto, Ontario. At that time, Thomas Keating said he hoped that some individuals who've practiced Centering Prayer and studied his work would elaborate on his ideas to develop them further. I found these remarks encouraging and decided to act on them.

So, building on the foundation of Thomas Keating's conceptual background for Centering Prayer, this book aims, from one particular viewpoint, to flesh out our basic instinctual needs, their distortions into emotional happiness programs, and the existential context in which we experience them. It also aims to indicate something of the liberating potential of our life and growth in God. The title, *Human Ground, Spiritual Ground: Paradise Lost and Found,* summarizes this. The book's contents come from not only study, reflection and observation of life, but also inspirations received and my own experience of the spiritual journey, with its ups and downs, inflations, deflations, illusions, and disillusionments regarding the false self and the true self.

Our spiritual journey includes all of life, everything we care about and in which we involve ourselves. My humble hope is that this book may be of some practical interest and use to others on the spiritual journey who are traveling some of the same inner terrain. Though it may be conceived and viewed in many ways, it is, after all, a terrain we all share. I don't feel I've developed Thomas Keating's core ideas any further here, but have added something to them, along with other basic ideas that place Centering Prayer's conceptual background in the general context of our human ground.

*Kess Frey*
*February 1, 2011*

# Introduction

## I

The human condition has a number of universal defining characteristics that are shared by all people throughout the Earth. Among these universal characteristics are four parameters of human existence, our basic instinctual needs, cultural conditioning, and our quest for meaning and fulfillment in life. A detailed definition and description of these universal characteristics is the basis for the view of the human condition presented in this book, which seeks to describe the binding attachments and illusions of our false self, and something of the way beyond that bondage into the freedom of our true self.

As we shall see, the four parameters of human existence are alluded to in the famous biblical story of Adam and Eve, found in the second and third chapters of Genesis (2:15–3:24). These four parameters are, in brief: 1) death/change, 2) sex/desire, 3) free will facing good/evil choices, and 4) our innate existential aloneness/incompleteness apart from God, the spiritual ground of our individual soul or energy-field. Each human being and society has to deal with these four basic parameters. They are defining characteristics and unavoidable limits of the human condition we all share.

Our basic instinctual needs are as old as humanity and, like the human soul or psyche, have roots in the history of life's evolution on Earth and in our spiritual ground. These basic needs were identified and described in various ways by modern twentieth-century developmental psychologists such as Sigmund Freud, Erik Erikson, and Abraham Maslow. Freud describes these needs in terms of the psychosexual stages of development (oral, anal, latency/urethral, and phallic). Erikson identifies them in terms of relational psychosocial stages and Maslow articulated a hierarchy of human needs, beginning with our basic instinctual needs and culminating in meta-needs of a higher order leading to self-actualization and ego-transcendence.[1] In addition to these discoveries and theories, work in the field of transpersonal psychology by such pioneers as Carl Gustav Jung, Roberto Assagioli and philosopher Ken Wilber has linked the individual human ground dimension of human life and existence to our deeper spiritual ground.[2]

The view of the human condition presented in this book is very much inspired by the work of my teacher, Father Thomas Keating, and the conceptual background he has developed for the practice of Centering Prayer.[3] This prayer practice is a contemporary method for opening to the gift of contemplation or "resting in God" by consenting at ever-deepening levels to the divine presence and action in us and in our life. Thomas Keating's model of the human condition is an original creative synthesis of information and wisdom drawn from a variety of classical and contemporary sources, and, no doubt, from the inspiration of the Holy Spirit within Father Keating himself. These sources include, but are not limited to, his personal experience of the Christian spiritual journey, years of interreligious dialogue and in-depth study of psychology, anthropology, sociology, philosophy, religion, history, and modern science.[4] The legacy of Thomas Keating's teaching, through live presentations, books and in audio and video formats, has been aptly called "a life-giving treasure."[5]

Thomas Keating has interestingly said, "Psychology is the handmaid of spirituality"—spirituality in this context being our relationship to God and the spiritual journey to inner wholeness and divine union. In his model of the human condition, Father Thomas identifies three primary basic instinctual needs we are all born with. These are 1) security/survival/safety, 2) affection/esteem/approval and 3) power/control. These needs must be met to some degree if we are to survive, grow and experience wellbeing in life. When these needs are not adequately met in early life, or are experienced as not met, due to neglect, abuse, or imagination, we suffer profound psychological trauma and wounding, as will be explained in this book. Unlike many of our desires, our true needs are not optional choices. This is what makes them needs and distinguishes them from other desires.

The damage of early life wounding related to our basic needs intensifies existential parameter four of the human condition, our innate
sense of aloneness/incompleteness apart from God and our spiritual
ground. As the trauma and pain of early life wounding are repressed
into unconscious areas of our energy-field, drives to compensate for
our felt losses are set up in the energy centers of our basic instinctual
needs. Thomas Keating aptly calls these unconscious drives to compensate "emotional programs for happiness that can't possibly work."
These unconscious happiness programs tend to run our life and form
the energetic core of what Fr. Thomas calls "the homemade self" or
"false-self system." This false self is our sense of separate-self identity
that emerges as we pass through the various developmental stages
and struggles leading up to puberty and beyond. Our false self is an
unavoidable and necessary development that tends to become overly
self-centered and compelled to pursue the particular unconscious programs for happiness that form its inner core.

The false self is a serious case of mistaken identity. It is who we
generally think we are but not who we really are as children of God
created in the divine image. The false self tends to experience itself as
utterly separate from God, though it may, at times, experience touches
of the divine as well as various delusions of grandeur. The false self
keeps us stuck in our human ground and generally functions as the
primary obstacle preventing us from realizing our spiritual ground's
divine potential. This tends to be the case because it's our false self
that motivates us toward egocentric selfishness and to actions contrary to universal spiritual values.

The false self and its emotional programs for happiness function
within the context of the four basic parameters of human existence
(death/change, sex/desire, good/evil choices, and our innate separate-
self feelings of aloneness/incompleteness). These existential boundaries make the false self's situation all the more poignant, desperate and
ultimately hopeless, especially existential parameter one, the inevitability of change and physical death. Consequently, the false self goes
to great lengths to avoid experiencing the reality of its dilemma. It
tends to, as Thomas Keating says, "rationalize, justify and glorify"
its projects for happiness. In doing so, the false self wants to escape

the truth of its tenuous position and thus involves itself in a variety of distractions, dramas and self-delusions, most of which revolve around its emotional programs for happiness and its relations to others.

In contrast to the false self, we have our true self and the quest of the spiritual journey. This quest involves honestly accepting and adapting to the full reality of our human existence as both human ground and spiritual ground. Its fulfillment involves discovering and, with God's help, becoming our true self, which is the only true solution to the dilemmas posed by our false self, our basic instinctual needs and the four parameters of human existence. The authentic spiritual journey requires an outgrowing and death of the false self in exchange for the gradual or sudden emergence into consciousness of our divine potential or true self. The basic goal is to bring about a shifting in our existential center of gravity and identity from the false self of our human ground to the true self of our spiritual ground, ultimately integrating the true self into our identity in human ground.

This dramatic transformation process is accomplished within us by divine grace working in concert with our humble and willing consent and cooperation. It is not something we can bring about on our own (as the false self) but is the work of God's presence and action in us and in our life. It requires growing faith and trust in God, and willingness to let go of whatever hinders our openness to the divine presence and action in our self, our life, and our relationships.

II

A further dimension of the false self, as explained by Thomas Keating, includes our over-identification with cultural conditioning and various groups in society to which we belong. This is the collective or communal dimension of the false self, beginning with our family of origin and extending to ethnic, racial, religious, social, economic, entertainment, national, political, peer, sexual, personal and other groups with which we may identify. Like our basic instinctual needs, which we inherit from Nature as part of God's divine plan, our cultural conditioning and various group identifications are necessary and unavoidable aspects of human life. We inherit them from previous and current generations for better or worse as a necessary part of becoming functioning members of our culture and society.

Cultural conditioning and group identifications play essential roles in each individual's physical, emotional, mental, psychic, social, and spiritual life, growth, and survival. Like our false self's emotional happiness programs that exaggerate and distort our basic instinctual needs, the full effects and extent of the influence exerted upon us by cultural conditioning and group identifications are generally not known to us. We become so identified with our false self, its happiness programs, cultural conditioning and various group identifications that we take these things for granted as part and parcel of who and what we inherently are. Consequently, we are often unable to separate ourselves from them in consciousness and view them objectively.

In the relative sense of our individual human identity, there is undeniable truth in the idea that our cultural conditioning and group identifications are part and parcel of whom and what we are. Cultural conditioning and group identifications form an integral part of our human ground. We need this sense of individual identity to feel grounded, oriented and secure in human life and society. However, in the deeper sense of our spiritual ground and identity in God, our cultural conditioning, and group identifications are not who and what we ultimately are as living souls created in the divine image. We are human beings and we are spiritual beings. The title of this book points toward this important truth.

Because all human groups and institutions are made up of people with false selves, it's inevitable that everyone's cultural conditioning and group identifications will contain flawed elements that are not in harmony with universal spiritual values of love, truth and freedom for all. Consequently, as Thomas Keating teaches, over-identification with our cultural conditioning and particular group tends to hold us back from realizing our true self. Such over-identification with our culture and group is a major obstacle to spiritual growth that must be outgrown if we're to complete the spiritual journey to interior freedom and union with God.

This is especially the case when the beliefs, values, prejudices, and worldviews of our cultural conditioning and group identifications reinforce the false self and conflict with authentic spiritual values. For example, ideological fanaticism and misplaced loyalty to any cause or group are lethal blinders that may prejudice our judgment, constrict our freedom and cloud our consciousness with delusions of exclusivity, superiority and self-righteousness. Such limitations trap us into a kind of false-self group-consciousness that opposes both spiritual growth and our human freedom.

It's important to bear in mind that God, or non-created Reality, is neither subject to nor defined by our cultural conditioning and group identifications, as we so frequently tend to be. The various contents of cultural conditioning and our group identifications (including our ideas of God) are, after all, limited human creations. They serve a legitimate purpose in our life and society; but at some point, we need to go beyond them, if we are to realize our true self and know the divine directly.

### III

For purposes of this book, we shall add two basic instinctual needs to the primary three identified by Thomas Keating (security/survival/safety, affection/esteem/approval and power/control). Our two additional needs are contained within Fr. Keatings' presentations but I want to focus particular attention and emphasis on them in this book. These two additional basic instinctual needs are 1) sensation/pleasure and 2) intimacy/belonging.

Since various kinds of sensation/pleasure are experienced in conjunction with gratification of all our basic needs and other desires, sensation/pleasure may easily be considered as a secondary or derived instinctual need, a kind of by-product of other needs. However, since both human wellbeing and the will to live require a certain amount of enjoyment, fun, humor and appreciation of life's goodness, it also seems reasonable to regard sensation/pleasure as a basic instinctual need in its own right. Healthy sensation/pleasure helps us to value our life by affirming the many gifts of human ground. Various experiences of sensation/pleasure may inspire us with gratitude and appreciation for life's awesome wonder, beauty, and goodness, affirming the everyday gifts and miracle of life and God's holy creation.

The second basic need we are here adding to Thomas Keating's original three is intimacy/belonging. Intimacy/belonging springs from our spiritual ground and is both an outer and inner need, both a social need and a spiritual need. It is our deepest need and our highest need because it connects us to all we care about. Intimacy/belonging is essentially our need for love, connecting us to our self, to others, to our culture and society, and ultimately to God. Hence, it includes our cultural conditioning, group identifications and much more.

## IV

The biblical story of Adam and Eve is used as a take-off point for discussing and interpreting the human condition in this book. The mythic theme of our lost paradise of primal intimacy/belonging, and the four limiting parameters of human existence alluded to in Genesis 2:15–3:24, supply us with apt metaphors for our discussion. Adam and Eve's expulsion from the Garden of Eden has, since the time of Saint Augustine of Hippo (AD 354-430), come to be associated with Original Sin, and is known as "the fall" of humanity from Paradise into our loss of innocence and intimacy with God. It is our fall from spiritual ground into human ground.

Accordingly, we shall refer to the four parameters of the human condition (death/change, sex/desire, good/evil choices, and our innate existential aloneness/incompleteness apart from God) as the "Fruits of the Fall." There has long been controversy surrounding the Adam and Eve story and the fall. Our situation of having to eat and digest the four fruits—that is, deal with these unavoidable existential parameters—may be interpreted, in terms of the Adam and Eve story, as what God intended or as the unintended consequence of Original Sin. It may also be seen as both of these interpretations.

The archetypal myth of Adam and Eve and their expulsion from Paradise is known the world over and its rich symbolism has been given many meanings and interpretations, ranging from the literal to

the figurative, from the moral and social to the psychological, theo-
logical and spiritual.[6] All interpretations of the Adam and Eve story
shed light on its amazing psychological symbolism. This story has
exerted powerful influences on human societies, civilizations, and
relationships throughout much of recorded history.

The ancient myth of Adam and Eve is pregnant with meanings
that speak deeply to all of us as both human beings and spiritual
beings. It is an intimate part of our individual and collective stories,
if we choose to regard it so. As primordial myths contain and may
reveal symbolic spiritual and psychological truths that are inacces-
sible to objective dualistic logic, one purpose of using the Adam and
Eve story in this book is to help us get some deeper intuitive feeling for
the actual human condition we all share and experience individually
and collectively.

V

The Fruits of the Fall are the above four unavoidable parameters
of human existence. These boundaries frame the existential context wherein we experience and pursue the gratification of our basic
instinctual needs and our self-chosen or culturally programmed
desires. The functioning and interrelations of the four Fruits of the
Fall, together with our five basic instinctual needs (including cultural
conditioning), form the perspective for the overall view of the human
condition presented in this book.

The aim of this book is threefold: 1) to articulate the four Fruits
of the Fall and our basic instinctual needs; 2) to describe and explain
some of the major obstacles to our spiritual growth in the context of
human ground; and 3), to give some indication of how we may outgrow our spiritual obstacles with the help of God's grace working in
us and in our life, and what this could be like (Paradise Found). In pursuing these basic three aims, this book seeks to describe the dynamic
living relationship between human ground and spiritual ground.

A central theme in this book is that we are human beings and
spiritual beings with earthly roots and heavenly roots. From our
earthly roots and the evolutionary life-force energy within us come

our instinctual needs, human personality and separate-self sense. The external influences of culture and society are also part of our earthly roots. From our heavenly roots come our spiritual potential and the impetus to evolve into more refined realms of consciousness with the divine image in our soul.

There is a natural tension between our earthly roots and our heavenly roots that manifests as inner conflict between our false self and our true self. It is an aim of this book to explain this conflict from its origins to its ending as we journey from our false self into our true self. The fact that we possess relative free will and attractions to both good and evil is pivotal to our spiritual drama and journey.

Engaging this book's subject matter calls for some thoughtful reflection, not only on its contents but on our personal history, involvement and experiences of life, especially looking at what we care about and what we want. This book seeks to mirror and explore the inner nature of our various human desires and strivings, their consequences for us, and the choices we face in pursuing them. Again, our aim here is to describe the universal human condition in terms of four existential parameters, our basic instinctual needs, and their distortions into a false-self system with emotional programs for happiness. We also intend to mention the healthy true-self alternative to the false self and its limitations.

PART ONE

# THE FALL AND ITS FRUITS

"So God created humankind in his image,
In the image of God he created them;
male and female he created them."

Genesis 1:27

# 1

## Our Lost Paradise

### I

$S$omewhere deep inside our heart, way back in our mind, perhaps buried in the unconscious, there's a nostalgic longing for a happy, intimate paradise we once knew, felt or imagined. It's a profound aching homesickness for what we miss most deeply, the fullness of our own heart's treasure lost in unconsciousness. Perhaps we felt it briefly as a child, toddler, or teen, or as an infant nursing at mother's breast. Maybe it dates back to a time in the womb where all was well in cozy comfort; we had all we needed and enjoyed feeling wanted, loved, and secure. Or, earlier still, could it be some primal cellular memory of our orgasmic conception with the wild spirit in sex erupting in timeless bliss of life's pure springing fountains?[1] Or possibly our happy, intimate paradise is an intuition or memory vibrating softly in our heart's echo canyon, whispering of where our spirit was before conception and the process of incarnation began?

Whatever it is, this nostalgia for a lost state of wellbeing, intimacy and happiness, for our own heart's treasure and former paradise, is a core archetype and dramatic theme inherent to the human condition we all share. As we awaken to consciousness in human life, somewhere deep inside us there's a sense of something missing, something vital and essential. We may feel this as an intuition or longing for a nondescript ideal state of happiness, intimacy, ease and wellbeing, a state that we know exists for us. We often experience this as children, glimpsing visions and tasting it in magical, carefree moments. These peak experiences tend to come at times when we're at peace and absorbed into the now-moment; when we feel loved, content, nourished by life or are simply having a good time and greatly enjoying being alive.

As we grow up and older, our vision of paradise typically fades or changes from its original innocence and simplicity into something more complex and conditioned by culture and society. We absorb without question the values and views of those around us and adjust our course in life accordingly. Sometimes we do this at great cost to our self because our original ideas of paradise and happiness have to be abandoned and sacrificed to gods of practicality, conformity, and realism; and may be replaced by other ideals and goals that don't really work for us. In a consumer society focused on the external and the material, we're taught to want more and more. We experience our selves as empty solitaries. Life becomes lonely, so we seek a sense of identity, security, and belonging in personal relationships, and in various groups to which we cling and conform.

We may pursue a way back to our lost paradise through intimate relationships involving sex, romance, and love. Such wonderful drama, fun and excitement makes life momentarily meaningful and entertaining, perhaps giving us brief intimations of what we so deeply desire, if not actual experiences of the warmth, bliss and thrills of heart's treasure to find. Or we may pursue our heart's satisfaction through friendships, approval, community and a sense of purpose in life. Feelings of place and belonging, of home and family, are often central to our inarticulate quest for paradise as happiness and wellbeing.

These outer pursuits and others symbolize and may complement an inner spiritual quest calling us to find what's missing in our self and what we need for inner wholeness. Wherever we find the good, the true and the beautiful, we are reminded intuitively of this quest for heart's treasure, connecting us to our Source and true home. We may not realize it consciously, but something close and true within us knows and responds instinctively and longingly to its reflections in the outer world.

The outer reflects the inner. Hence, all beauty can touch us deeply, be it primarily natural, aesthetic, moral, physical, sexual or spiritual. For example, our sexual desire is what it is on its own level; that is, it may be impersonal or personal lust, hunger, and addiction, desire for fun and play, or longing for intimacy in adoration of the beloved. At the same time, on deeper levels, our sexuality and desire are primarily a spiritual allegory expressing 1) the mystery of creation, 2) our conscious self's longing for wholeness of soul, and 3) our deep inner self's longing for inner union with the divine beloved.

Deep within us, usually in unconscious depths of our energy-field, our inner self knows that we can find lasting wholeness only in union with the divine, represented by our complementary feminine or masculine opposite. Actually, our soul's complementary feminine or masculine opposite (anima or animus) lies within us, hidden in the unconscious recesses of our energy-field. However, we typically tend to see it reflected in the outer world around us, in some special person to whom we feel irresistibly attracted and with whom we may fall helplessly in love via unconscious projection of our romantic/spiritual ideal. This theme has been explored and discussed at length by Jungian analyst Robert A. Johnson in *We,* his illuminating book on the psychology of romantic love.[2]

In *We,* Mr. Johnson points out the telling fact that a good part of Western Civilization, in its eager embrace of scientific materialism and its cynical rejection of religion, has become spiritually numb and blind. Consequently, for some people, falling in love via unconscious projection of their anima or animus onto another person is the only way open to them for consciously engaging the numinous realm of the soul's sacred dimension and inner depths. Unfortunately, such unconscious projections, through which the soul tries to awaken us to its sacred dimension, generally lead to disappointment and disillusionment due to ignorance of our inner life and unrealistic expectations regarding the idealized other person. This letdown, in turn, may reinforce one's cynicism regarding love and the divine.

In falling in love, we may wonder, is it simply the other person that bowls us over and captures our heart? Or is it the image of our complementary opposite reflected in the person of the beloved that so completely wins us over? There's a psychological and spiritual secret to romantic, sexual love's awesome power to possess and obsess. It is this: what we fall so madly in love with is actually our soul's own reflection. That is, we fall for the contra-sexual image, our ideal complementary opposite unconsciously projected onto the beloved, who possesses the appropriate qualities and characteristics to call forth and carry our projection. The attraction is so compelling because it's actually an unconscious expression of our soul's deepest longing for wholeness and divine union. Hence, the beloved appears to embody our soul's Lost Paradise. He or she is unconsciously chosen as an object of projection by something deep inside us.

This is one secret of love's deep mystery, an important secret of falling in love, but not the full story. It never is, for all we can say and dream of love is limited to the skies of our mind's conceptions, and love knows no horizons. Love is broader than space, boundless as the lost deep flowing beyond life's first light. Love's deep mystery plays in many ways through all hearts and patterns of relationship. It is the silent breath of God binding all together in unity of the eternal divine, for, as scripture tells us, "God is love" (1 John 4:7–8) and love is God. The divine love of non-created Reality is our true home from before creation. Our soul's innate longing for this love is its "homing instinct." It is our deepest and strongest yearning for our Lost Paradise of primal intimacy. All other desires we may perceive or pursue as ultimate are but pale substitutes.

Deep down, in the true center of our being, we all have a burning inner longing for connection and relatedness to the eternal divine. The ideal of "Paradise," the perfect place, however we may conceive it, is symbolic of this. Thus, the quest for our Lost Paradise is more than an inchoate desire to return to the carefree joys of childhood, to the bliss of mother's breast or the oceanic oneness, security and comfort of the womb. It's more than our powerful unconscious longing to return to the orgasmic unity and ecstasy of life's pure springing fountains imprinted in our primeval psyche (soul) and cellular organism at the moment of conception. It is ultimately our quest for God, the eternal Source and ground of our being.

We may conceive of God or the divine in many ways; all of which are imperfect. I like to think of God as "Ultimate Mystery" or "non-created Reality." These terms suggest something intimately close that's yet impossible for us to accurately or fully comprehend, articulate, or imagine. Our inner quest for the eternal divine is the religious quest for our origins, for the deepest center of our soul's energy-field and Source of being. It is our quest for spiritual growth and realization of our divine potential. The quest for happiness, for our Lost Paradise, however we may pursue it, starts us on this journey.

## II

Our soul's "homing instinct," our deep spiritual desire to return consciously to our Source, is inspired by the spirit in creation as love divided seeking reunion. To return consciously to non-created Reality, we and the yearning spirit of life within us need to evolve forward in time through created reality to fulfill the divine plan of creation, rather than "returning" by regressing backward whence we came into oblivion and unconsciousness. This is a key point regarding the two paths of good and evil (existential parameter three) and where they ultimately take us. This vital spiritual topic will be discussed later in this book.

The divine wholeness of eternal love in non-created Reality is the "Lost Paradise" of our deepest spiritual yearning, which is essentially the energy of God's love in us divided and seeking reunion. Hence, the evolutionary spirit of life and creation in us is the primal origin of the "Lost Paradise Archetype," and of all subsequent desires we may experience. That is, the spirit of love divided seeking reunion is creation's deepest and ultimate yearning. It is the origin and inspiration of all our various inborn and acquired needs and desires for pleasure and fulfillment, for the completion of all images conceived in our mind and dreamed in our heart as goals to be attained, be they great or small.

the Lost Paradise Archetype is a universal theme in human life and psychology. This archetype has both spiritual and physiological roots in the human soul and organism (roots in spiritual ground and human ground). The spiritual dimension of the Lost Paradise Archetype in us derives from the primal intimacy of our individual energy-field's origins; that is, the birth or coming to be of our individual soul in God's eternal love. This mysterious process is the origin of the divine life force within us and of our individual soul. It is the beginning of the great adventure into incarnation where the divine energy of non-created Reality sets forth into the vicissitudes and uncertainties of created reality as individual energy-fields of evolving life and consciousness. We are each a part of this great adventure.

The Lost Paradise of our spiritual origins is imprinted in the soul as primal memory. Similarly, the Lost Paradise of our physiological origins, from conception and formation in the womb through birth, nursing, and conscious emergence into human incarnation, is imprinted in the brain as core memory. The healthy spiritual and physiological aspects of the Lost Paradise Archetype blend together into a heart of kindness as love, care, intimacy, comfort, and tenderness. These qualities in those who care for us play essential roles in our nurturing into human life. As helpless infants and sensitive, impressionable children, we are dependent on others for our care and education, and we remain vulnerable to deep wounding in our needs to thrive and survive. Let us hope and pray that love's mercy and grace may guide and protect all souls born into created reality through those who care for them.

So, the spiritual and physiological roots of the Lost Paradise Archetype are grounded first in our soul's experience before incarnation, then in our physical formation process in the womb and in our experiences of comfort, care and intimacy as infants clinging to our mother. All of these experiences, like everything else in time, are temporary and we are forced by Nature to leave them. Leaving them and not wanting to is the experiential basis of the Lost Paradise Archetype. Every comfortable position we have to leave in human life but don't want to leave is a symbolic replay of the primary Lost Paradise Archetype imprinted in our energy-field or psyche. This Lost Paradise Archetype is a primary expression of human life's first existential parameter: death/change. It also ties directly into the second parameter, sex/desire, as we try to recover our Lost Paradise.

Thus, the Lost Paradise Archetype pertains to all temporary states that we enjoy in varying degrees, wish to remain in, but are unable to keep or sustain as long as we'd like. Hence, the Lost Paradise Archetype is a paradigm of the human condition's enduring impermanence under basic existential parameter one (death/change). We experience this archetype whenever we don't want to get up out of bed, leave a nice warm shower or an intimate embrace. It's there when we come to the end of any pleasure or delight in human life and its pull is part of what drives us to desire more and more in attempting to recapture what we've lost.

the Lost Paradise Archetype always involves a carefree, contented state we'd like to regain, escape into, and remain in, enjoying peace, comfort, intimacy, laughter, drama, pleasure or excitement. I'm sure we can all think of many examples from our own experience. the Lost Paradise Archetype is an inevitable and necessary part of human existence that impels us to change and grow.

This archetype takes expression on all levels of our being and experience, from our human ground to our spiritual ground. Our failure to come to terms with it; that is, to accept the temporary nature of everything in created reality causes much suffering and unhappiness in human life. In this way, the Lost Paradise Archetype intensifies our experiences of existential aloneness/incompleteness (parameter four), motivating us to seek lasting intimacy, wholeness, peace and love. Thus, it ultimately serves a higher purpose by prodding our soul's yearning quest for the eternal divine, once we become aware that the quest exists.

## III

We hungry humans frequently pursue our Lost Paradise in the concrete desires and delights of the flesh, as, for example, in various sensory pleasures and erotic sexuality, seeking the permanent in the fleeting, preferring at least a taste to nothing at all. There's a universal symbolism encoded in the soul where erotic sexuality symbolizes the union of all opposites. The ideal fantasy of erotic sexuality as something to be desired evokes more than images and hopes of sensory thrills and pleasure. On deeper levels, it evokes the promise of naked transparency and self-disclosure, mutual acceptance, passion, intimacy, vulnerability, tenderness, and caring love; all associated with our Lost Paradise.

The embrace of sexual union symbolizes all unions. Nakedness symbolizes full self-disclosure and the longed-for embrace of sexual union holds promise of welcome for our incomplete separate-self into a temporary paradise of acceptance, love, and fulfillment shared with another person. This, at least, is the lost-paradise ideal and appeal of erotic sexuality, which, in imaging a longed for union, symbolizes the fulfillment of all our desires. Hence, the second existential parameter of human life is called "sex/desire."

The welcoming embrace of a lover heralds immediate acceptance, intimacy, pleasure and an end to painful isolation and loneliness, or so we may hope. Whether it is conscious or unconscious, reality or illusion in actual fact, this is what erotic sexuality symbolizes in the human psyche. The intimacy of the body is a return to the primal intimacy of our beginnings in this world. It's a return to the slimy splendor and Lost Paradise of our time in the womb, our time on the breast and our awakening into life. In other words, the intimacy of the body has a deep meaning for us that takes us back to our origins in this life.

The well-known biblical story of Adam and Eve (Genesis 2:7–3:24) gives a good expression of the Lost Paradise Archetype, pointing toward the basic human ground and condition we all share. The Garden of Eden is a timeless paradise of peace, harmony and plenty. Adam and Eve enjoyed a life of unconscious innocence in Nature and intimacy with God in this garden, until they ate the forbidden fruit. This forbidden fruit grows on "the tree of the knowledge of good and evil," which grows in the garden near the "Tree of Life," or immortality (Genesis 3:22), "in the midst of the garden" (Genesis 2:9).

Why did they eat the fruit of the "knowledge of good and evil" tree when God had warned them not to? Tempted by a talking Serpent and seduced by curiosity (something inherent to human nature), Eve, the receptive feminine principle in the human soul, "saw that the tree was good for food." She saw "that it was a delight to the eyes, and that the tree was to be desired to make one wise; she took of its fruit and ate" (Genesis 3:6). How she, in her innocent, unknowing state, was able to see this we are not told—some intuition perhaps. After tasting it, Eve gave the forbidden fruit to her husband, the then innocent and naïve masculine principle in human nature. As the story goes, once Adam and Eve had both eaten of this fruit, "the eyes of both were opened and they knew that they were naked." In other words, they underwent a dramatic change in consciousness regarding their sexuality. Thus the forbidden fruit was a kind of psychoactive substance. Eating it caused them to feel separate, to see things differently, and to experience embarrassment or shame regarding exposed genitals. When "they knew that they were naked; they sewed fig leaves together and made loincloths for themselves" (Genesis 3:7).

I find it curious that, in the story, Eve's eyes were not "opened" immediately when she ate of the forbidden fruit. It was only after both had eaten that "their eyes were opened." Perhaps both feminine and masculine elements of the soul had to experience the forbidden fruit before the change in consciousness or loss of childlike innocence could take place? What was or is the experience of this change in consciousness like? The uncomfortable feeling of being exposed naked, whether physically or otherwise, carries with it, for many of us, a learned sense of embarrassment and shame, just as it spontaneously did for Adam and Eve after they ate the forbidden fruit. This is especially apparent in our socially and culturally conditioned attitudes regarding sex in general and the genitals in particular.

Adam and Eve's experience in the story and their attempts to cover up represent all such experiences we may have, as children or adults, when we "see that we're naked." That is, when we realize we're exposed, have done something wrong, been found out or feel we've something to be ashamed of that we want to hide or cover up. In this story and its implications, we again see the central and important role of sexual symbolism in human life and drama, where Adam and Eve's exposed genitals represent anything and everything we may feel guilty about, ashamed of or want to hide. Before they ate the forbidden fruit and their eyes were opened, Adam and Eve were innocent and had no idea or sense of shame and nakedness.

## IV

The talking Serpent that persuaded Eve to try the forbidden fruit is a symbol of many meanings.[3] It represents something powerful and profound in the human psyche. The biblical Serpent is a primary expression of what we may call the "divine life force" within us. The Serpent may be seen as a phallic symbol representing creation's primal life-force energy, including our quests for sexuality, curiosity, desire, knowledge and wisdom.[4] It has also been widely regarded as the symbol or embodiment of Satan, "the adversary," "tempter" or "evil one."

For better or worse, the Serpent impels us to learn from personal experience by trying new things and discovering their painful or pleasurable consequences. The Serpent, elongated in space, is also a symbol of time, where knowledge is gained through experience. It is in time that creation's evolution takes place, and it was into time, as we now know it, that Adam and Eve (humanity) fell upon their expulsion from Paradise.

The talking Serpent in the Garden, who was subsequently silenced (pushed down into the unconscious) and cursed by God to crawl in the dust of Earth and be enemies with Eve's children, is a mysterious, potent and pregnant symbol. This Serpent introduces essential elements of conflict and drama into the biblical story of creation and humanity's plight on Earth. It embodies a core ingredient of human nature, a kind of tragic flaw that's necessary for our evolution and growth as human beings and spiritual beings. In this light, it makes sense to suppose, as C. G. Jung suggests,[5] that what occurred in the Garden of Eden and its consequences for humanity were actually the all-knowing, all-powerful God's intentions from the beginning. There are, of course, differing and conflicting opinions regarding this question.

Though it's a virtual paradise of intimacy, innocence and plenty, the Garden of Eden is a kind of timeless, unconscious holding state where nothing really changes. Life there is easy and no struggle, drama, or evolution may take place until after a decision is made to go against the rules laid down by the boss, who in this case is God. Were Adam and Eve, as Jung suggests, unwittingly programmed or set-up to make this decision and try the forbidden fruit? It seems to me most likely so and that the human condition, wonderful, beautiful, pleasurable, painful, and problematic as it is, was divinely intended to be our lot.

In any case, this fateful choice, or even its possibility, introduces the element of human free will, a free will that is somewhat limited, conditioned, and predetermined by need and Nature but that, nonetheless, has at least the appearance of reality. Free will, our belief in the capacity to make conscious decisions, is essential for imagining any meaningful life, drama or personal relationships above the mechanical level of instinctual compulsion and automatic programming. Our relative "free will" makes human life and relationships interesting, meaningful, and somewhat unpredictable.

Human free will is obviously an essential part of the divine plan for our evolution and growth as human beings and spiritual beings. If it was God's intention for Adam and Eve to exercise free will by eating the forbidden fruit, then the Serpent that gave them this suggestion is really not so bad or evil. It is, in fact, an agent of the divine will, created by God and placed in the Garden for this very purpose. Like the wild sexuality and all else it symbolizes, the biblical Serpent is a necessary antagonist in our existential drama. Without it, there would be no evolutionary life force or human condition as we now know and experience them.

The primal Serpent's creative energy gives rise to our instinctual nature and to all our desires, which we, to some degree, may choose and direct with our relative free will. Hence the Serpent is a primary expression of creation's life-force energy as understood in this book. When our instinctual desire nature is repressed or goes to extremes and gets out of control, it becomes a deadly poison that leads us to destruction. Yet this poison, which we tend to fear so much, can also be curative and life giving, when used appropriately and wisely. That is, when the Serpent's raw instinctual energy within us is directed into healthy channels of moderation and balance via right use of our relative free will, it produces art, culture, civilization, morality, religion, and higher states of consciousness. Thus the Serpent of temptation also represents our evolutionary potential and progress.

Humanly and spiritually speaking, the unconscious state of being dominated by instinctual desires, habitual patterns, and blind conformity is about as commendable as slavery. Without free will and consciousness to exercise it, we have no individual freedom, our life is bereft of existential meaning, and there's no opportunity to evolve forward into higher states of being. Adam and Eve's primal act of disobedience was necessary to begin the process of evolution. Its consequences (fruits) are the four existential parameters of the human condition with which we all have to contend.

One of these consequences is the inevitable conflict between good and evil in human life and nature (existential parameter three). We all face this conflict, both individually and collectively. The price of our growth into spiritual freedom is the need to confront and overcome all evil motivations, tendencies and slothful inertia in our energy-field that oppose our progress into spiritual awakening. It is precisely this struggle that makes us grow stronger and wiser, as through it and the bitter experiences that often accompany it we learn firsthand the knowledge of good and evil. In this light, we may regard the Serpent of temptation as a beloved opponent, teacher, or antagonist, rather than as simply "the evil one." As we struggle against and, with help from above, overcome the evil that opposes us, we evolve into fuller states of being and awareness. Then the lowly instinctual Serpent pent-up within us gradually transforms into a soaring eagle spreading its wings in the free open sky of our growing spiritual awakening. This liberating return of our soul to its Lost Paradise in God is the ultimate fulfillment and awakening of the biblical Serpent, divine life force or spirit of love divided seeking reunion. It is the evolution and awakening of our instinctual human ground into our divine spiritual ground.

## V

Apparently Adam and Eve did not have sexual relations until after they'd eaten the forbidden fruit on "the tree of the knowledge of good and evil" and had been expelled from Paradise (Genesis 4:1). In the garden, they were innocent in their nakedness, as the Serpent of erotic sexuality and creation's evolutionary life force was not yet active within them but was perceived as external to them in their consciousness. That is, like the Lord God, it was experienced as a kind of projection and separate, outside entity that spoke to them.

This pattern is repeated in each human life where both God and the spirit of evolving life and creation are initially perceived in human consciousness as being external to the self. The Serpent's reproductive power sleeps in our unconscious as we pass through infancy and childhood. Gradually, we emerge from the playful familiarity and innocence of childhood into the sharper, harsher reality of our separate-self consciousness and the four Fruits of the Fall. As puberty approaches, the legendary Serpent of sexuality begins to stir within us, bringing sudden dramatic changes in body and soul. Thus begins our searching quest in darkness and light for happiness, wholeness and our Lost Paradise.

As we pass through adolescence into young adulthood, sexuality looms large as a visible or invisible giant gorilla in the living room of our conscious awareness. We may choose to acknowledge or deny its presence, but we can't escape its influence. It's loose in our energy-field raising restless surges of erotic energy, urgency, and desire in body and soul. The libido of desire pounds in our brain and blood as a drumbeat of motivation to do something, to scratch our restless itch, to get what we want.

However, what do we want? This is a question of existential choice each person must continue answering throughout life. Our menu of options is full as a modern supermarket with no empty shelves. There are plenty of messages that come from near and far suggesting what we need or ought to desire.

## VI

As mentioned previously, sexual union is a natural symbol for regaining our Lost Paradise and for the fulfillment of our desires. Sexual union expresses the image of joining two into one (wholeness) while also involving a return of our energies and awareness to the place of our physical origins and birth. On the deepest level, sexual desire and union are also symbolic expressions of our soul's "homing instinct" for the Lost Paradise of its divine origins.

The symbolic psychic association of sex with fulfillment in general may be largely unconscious, but it draws and attracts us with a lure that's hard to resist. This psychological fact is well known to advertisers who often associate their advertised products with pleasure, intimacy, fulfillment and rewards linked to sex that in truth have nothing to do what they're trying to sell us. Some commercials and subliminal messages even go so far as to associate the desires and fulfillment of human relationships, intimacy, and sex with inanimate objects like computers, electronics, telecommunication equipment, and cars.

On the inner spiritual level, outer sexual attraction, desire, and union are symbolic of what takes place inside us when we become whole and united to our deep inner self in spiritual ground. This does not require the realization of some ideal vision of sexual union with another person happening in our life, as external desires may lead us to believe. Such fulfillment is not the point here. The main, most relevant and liberating point here is that the ideal sexual union of two human energy-fields is actually an outer symbol for what may take place within each of us in relation to the divine. Each individual human soul, or energy-field, possesses the divine Feminine and Masculine Principles within itself and may, with the love and help of God's grace, unite these principles or forces in its self to create experiences of inner transformation, spiritual awakening, and divine union.

Outer union is a metaphor for the sacred mystery of the inner mystical union that takes place through our soul's inner energy exchange with God, which gradually harmonizes and integrates all the energies of our being. It is this inner energy exchange with the divine, activated by grace via deep prayer, meditation, and worship, that gives us transformation, renewal and spiritual awakening. From a mystical perspective, outer sexual union is primarily a living symbol of our energy-field's coming into the inner healing, renewal and wholeness that create in our soul the restoration and fulfillment of our Lost Paradise and lost intimacy with God. This inner renewal is the awakening of the divine image within us.

The transformative possibility and fulfillment of our being in love is the Lost Paradise we naturally intuit and most deeply desire, unconsciously if not consciously. It is this deep spiritual yearning, projected and objectified into our outer life in relation to another person that can make erotic attraction and infatuation so deeply compelling. In other words, our soul's sexual desire is, on the deepest level, a symbolic expression of its yearning for God and divine union.

Hence, the real action of life and the spirit is not in the outer world's changing surface appearances and relationships, as we may believe. In truth, the ultimate action of life and in relation to God for each of us happens in our own soul. Our soul's energy-field is part of the One Divine-Energy-field and goes all the way back to God. This liberating vital point needs to be understood, utilized, and celebrated, for it is the deepest and most wonderful secret of our Lost Paradise, the divine life-force energy in us and the spiritual quest.

## 2

## FRUITS OF THE FALL

### I

The Fruits of the Fall are the four basic parameters of our existence in this world. They are universal boundaries that condition the existence of every human being. These fruits of our existence are a direct consequence of Adam and Eve's eating the forbidden fruit and being expelled from Paradise. Death/change, sex/desire, good/evil choices and our aloneness/incompleteness apart from God are all mentioned or alluded to in the Garden of Eden myth (Genesis 2:7– 3:24). And the Lord God commanded the man, "You may freely eat of every tree in the garden; but of the tree of the knowledge of good and evil you shall not eat, for in the day that you eat of it you shall die" (Genesis 2:16–17).

The above passage introduces existential parameters one, death/change, and three, good/evil choices. Persuaded by the know- ing Serpent and despite the Lord God's warning, Adam and Eve chose to try the forbidden fruit. The first thing they knew after eating the forbidden fruit was that they were naked (Genesis 3:7). This startling event introduces existential parameter two, sex/desire. It also associ- ates awareness of human sexuality with forbidden knowledge of good and evil. That is, it was the fruit of the tree of the knowledge of good and evil that brought about the change in consciousness that opened the eyes of Adam and Eve to the idea of embarrassment or shame in their nakedness.

The fourth Fruit of the Fall, our existential aloneness and incom- pleteness in being alienated from God, also comes as a consequence of disobeying the Lord God's command against eating the forbidden fruit. In going against what they understand to be God's will, Adam and Eve separate themselves from God by choosing to follow their own separate will in a different direction. As a result of this, they are cast out from the idyllic paradise of Eden into the human condition of death/change, sex/desire, suffering, loneliness, and good/evil fruits that we inhabit today. With separation from the Lord God comes our haunting sense of inner aloneness/incompleteness. Our natural response to this is to try and fill in the hole in our soul by pursuing various forms of sex/desire, the second Fruit of the Fall.

Regarding the forbidden fruit itself, the Lord God tells Adam, "in toil you shall eat of it all the days of your life; thorns and thistles it shall bring forth for you" (Genesis 3:17–18). In addition, the Lord God sent him forth from the Garden of Eden to till the ground from which he was taken. He drove out the man; and at the east of the Garden of Eden he placed a cherubim, with a sword flaming and turning to guard the way to the Tree of Life (Genesis 3:23–24). When the Lord God drove out the man, sent him away into the lonely, challenging, and troublesome human condition, this completed the fourth Fruit of the Fall. The emptiness referred to here is the pain of existential aloneness, uncertainty and incompleteness we suffer in feeling cut-off from God in the face of death/change, sex/desire and good/evil choices; that is, in the face of our human condition.

The biblical story of Adam and Eve communicates something that goes deeper than intellectual logic alone can comprehend. This story reaches deep into our intuitive unconscious. It has many layers of meaning and leaves much to our imagination. In what follows, we shall imagine some of these layers and use them to develop our vision of the human condition in terms of its four existential parameters. The several layers of meaning in the Adam and Eve story have, over time, naturally given rise to various interpretations or ways of understanding this story, ranging from the linear/historical to the archetypal/mythic. In what follows, I shall use those interpretations that seem to best serve our purpose in this book of describing the human condition.

The story of Adam and Eve is the Bible's explanation of our human condition, its origins and how our initial relationship to God came to be. Adam and Eve's disobedience of the Lord God's command in eating the forbidden fruit has been called "Original Sin."[1] And their expulsion from the Garden of Eden is commonly known as "the fall" of humanity from Paradise and intimacy with God into the "lost-paradise" human condition we inhabit today. Everyone who knows this story has her or his own responses to it, which may range from blind belief to curious interest to dismissing it as absurd to taking it quite seriously. In this book, I want to touch upon two basic kinds of interpretation of Original Sin and the fall. These I am calling "tragic interpretations" and "evolutionary interpretations." The reader is invited to draw her or his own conclusions regarding these interpretations.

## II

Surface readings of the Adam and Eve story easily lend themselves to tragic interpretations. In these understandings of the myth, the Original Sin of disobedience is seen as the fatal error leading to the fall. There was only one simple rule to obey and Adam and Eve had to go and break it! This stupid mistake, however innocently committed, is seen as the cause of two terrible interrelated situations. These are, 1) our loss of intimacy and security in relation to the Lord God, and 2) our being cast out from Eden into the challenges, difficulties, and misery of the human condition we know today as history and the current crises facing our world. The grossly inhumane abuses, brutality, and exploitations committed by various peoples against each other and inadvertently against Nature may be cited as convincing testimony for tragic interpretations of Original Sin and the fall.

When Adam and Eve (representing generic humanity) broke the one simple rule laid down by the Lord God, they had some help. It may never have occurred to them, in their unknowing state, to try the forbidden fruit, had not the crafty Serpent suggested this idea to them. In tragic views, the Serpent is clearly seen as the villain, the evil spoiler who messed things up and who is the enemy of humanity. The

Serpent in the Garden of Eden is an archetype of the original hustler, con artist, seducer, and trickster. Blame for the tragic outcomes of Original Sin and the fall is heaped upon the lowly despised Serpent, who misled Adam and Eve. Evolutionary interpretations, as we shall see, take a quite different view of the Serpent.

In the biblical text we read, the Lord God said to the Serpent, "Because you have done this, cursed are you among all animals and among all wild creatures; upon your belly you shall go, and dust you shall eat all the days of your life. I will put enmity between you and the woman, and between her offspring and yours; he will strike your head and you will strike his heel" (Genesis 3:14-15).

This clearly portends an adversarial relationship between humanity and the Serpent in the fallen state of the human condition that's about to follow in the story. If, as in evolutionary interpretations of the myth, the Serpent is understood to represent the instinctual life-force energy within us, the above passage portends a challenging if not adversarial relationship between human beings and the vital energies of instinct within us. This includes how we relate to and try to satisfy our basic instinctual needs.

The biblical passage continues as follows: To the woman he said, "I will greatly increase your pangs in childbearing; in pain you shall bring forth children, yet your desire shall be for your husband, and he shall rule over you" (Genesis 3:16). These words seem to express the Lord God's wrath toward Eve (woman), suggesting she will desire sexual relations with her husband in spite of painful childbirth. "He shall rule over you," suggests that the relationship between the sexes will be one of inequality. The above words of the Lord God allude to the fruit of sex/desire and definitely lend themselves to tragic interpretations of the fall since domination and inequality are inconsistent with true love and easily lead to conflict, suffering, and abuse in human relationships. The sad and pathetic tragedy of domestic violence in many families and intimate relationships may be cited as one unfortunate example of this.

The passage concludes as follows: And to the man he said, "Because you have listened to your wife, and have eaten of the tree about which I commanded you, 'You shall not eat of it,' cursed is the ground because of you; in toil you shall eat of it all the days of your life; thorns and thistles it shall bring forth for you; and you shall eat the plants of the field. By the sweat of your face you shall eat bread until you return to the ground, for out of it you were taken; you are dust and to dust you shall return" (Genesis 3:17–19).

The above words say much about the human condition that's about to follow in the wake of Original Sin and the fall. They stress the fruit of death/change and inequality of the sexes, which may be inferred from the Lord God chastising Adam (man) for listening to (trusting) the voice of his wife when she suggested eating the forbidden fruit with her. Eating the forbidden fruit, of course, is the main thing the Lord God acts so displeased about, as he says, "Cursed is the ground because of you." It's as if the Lord God is saying everything is ruined because of this shameful disobedience. Dire consequences must follow. No more free lunch!

In toil, humanity is to eat of the forbidden fruit of the tree of the knowledge of good and evil "all the days of your life." The "thistles and thorns" good and evil conflicts bring forth are the sufferings of the human condition. The human lot in the fallen state is to be one of labor and hardship, a painful struggle to survive until, at last, we die "and to dust you shall return." This all sounds like a grim tragic outcome for Adam and Eve (humanity) with no possibility for an afterlife or redemption.

As the scripture reads: "He drove out the man" (Genesis 3:24). This being driven out from the Garden, and from the Lord God's presence, is like a painful rejection and kind of spiritual death for Adam and Eve (humanity). This banishment becomes the fourth Fruit of the Fall and the origin of the powerful Lost Paradise Archetype discussed in the previous chapter. Adam and Eve (and we) are thus separated from the Lord God, Source of life, and from the wealth of immortal goodness arising within and flowing out from the divine presence.

The easy comforts of a beloved home and of conscious familiarity and closeness to the Lord God are both lost in the fall. This outcome of rejection and loss of the Lord God's favor may be seen as a painful heartbreaking tragedy with long-term consequences for all subsequent generations of suffering humanity. This loss is the wound in the souls of all humans that gives rise to our innate sense of existential aloneness/incompleteness. Thus we are haunted by an uncertain longing tied to the deep intuition and distant memory of our former Paradise in God.

On psychological grounds, Adam and Eve's expulsion from Paradise may be compared to the trauma of physical human birth. In this symbolic comparison, just as Adam and Eve were expelled from Paradise, so is every human infant expelled from the security and comforts of its mother's womb to become a helpless newborn entering our fallen human condition.[2] In the fall from Paradise, Adam and Eve went from carefree innocence, abundance, and security into uncertainty of survival and certainty of death. They fell from familiar intimacy with the Lord God into estrangement and loss of that easy relationship. This fall was a kind of spiritual death into feeling separate and apart from our life-giving Source. In human ground, we are all heirs to this spiritual death of feeling alone and apart from the holy inner ground of our being (our spiritual ground). Having been exiled from the Lord God's presence, Adam and Eve (humanity) have fallen under the sway of temptation to evil and become subject to the four Fruits of the Fall.

## III

If we relate to it, the biblical story of Adam, Eve, the Serpent, and the Lord God is really about each one of us, since each of us is heir to the fall and its fruits. Each of us is, to some degree, consciously or unconsciously identified with Adam and Eve as our primal parents. We are also, perhaps on deep intuitive levels, identified with the biblical Serpent or divine life force as the instinctual impetus and driving energy of will and desire within us. Consequently, we are emotionally involved with the story's contents in a profound, powerful way. This is because what happened to Adam and Eve in the biblical myth has, in a very real symbolic sense, also happened to each of us. That is, we are each cast out from our former Paradise of primal unity and subject to the Fruits of the Fall in human ground. We each long for our Lost Paradise of primal intimacy with the Lord God, and for resolution to our basic human predicament.

The Fruits of the Fall invariably bring us various degrees of alternating suffering and enjoyment. This basic pattern of experience has endless variations and is an inevitable characteristic of the human condition. We are all bound to cycles of suffering and enjoyment until we outgrow our foolish fallen nature (false self), transcend our childish illusions, and come into realization of our true self in God. The process of growth and awakening into our true self in God is generally one of gradual steps or degrees rather than a sudden dramatic all-at-once transformation. It unfolds as we continue to eat the fruit of the tree of the knowledge of good and evil growing in our human ground. To be human is to be subject to natural human limitations. It is to be capable of both good and evil and of experiencing suffering as well as enjoyment in human life. Experience is food for our soul.

The holding cup of our soul's energy-field is the inner receptacle of all our experiences and memories where they live on within us. This inner cup is gradually deepened and matured through intense experiences of enjoyment, suffering and growing self-knowledge. Through this deepening process, our outlook on life evolves. Consequently, we may outgrow our more superficial desires and begin to desire from deeper places within us, places closer to our spiritual ground and true self.

Whether or not we grow into harmony with our spiritual ground and true self in this life depends on how we respond to our various experiences of pleasure, pain, and growing self-knowledge. Sooner or later, the deepening of our soul's holding cup via joy, sorrow and self-knowledge renders each of us a deeper person capable of more powerful and profound emotional experience and understanding. This deepening process is central to our spiritual evolution, the implication being that all we go through and experience in life is ultimately nourishment for our soul's ongoing growth in compassion, wisdom and understanding.

## IV

Tragic views of the fall say that Adam and Eve's eating the forbidden fruit is not what was supposed to happen, that it was not the

Lord God's intention because the Lord God had forbidden it. These views are consistent with a literal, surface reading of the biblical text. Literal, tragic interpretations of the fall are also consistent with beliefs that human life entails suffering because of Adam and Eve's sins of pride and disobedience in wanting to become equal to God on their own terms (as opposed to God's terms). Consequently, the spiritual meaning or purpose of human life is often not thought of as evolutionary but as a test of obedience, involving our earning either eternal punishment or reward in the next life based on our behavior in this life.

Such fundamental beliefs are widespread and known to most of us. In these tragic interpretations of the fall, the archetypal pattern of obedience/disobedience leading to reward/punishment has three distinct phases. It begins first with Adam, Eve, the Serpent, and the Lord God in the Garden of Eden, where the initial disobedience took place. In the second phase, the drama continues here on Earth throughout each human life where we experience various temptations and must make good/evil choices. Finally, it concludes for each of us after physical death in an eternal afterlife where we receive our just deserts in either Heaven or Hell. This is a view commonly associated with absolute fundamentalist beliefs in the world's major theistic religions: Judaism, Christianity, and Islam. Many of us were taught these fundamentalist views involving eternal reward or punishment as children. Such absolute beliefs create a feeling of guaranteed certainty and security for the ego or separate-self, if one is sufficiently and properly obedient to what God requires of us in our dualistic relationship with Him.

Evolutionary views, on the other hand, generally see God, the Ultimate Mystery of non-created Reality, to be something infinitely more than a glorified parent figure who rewards and punishes us for good or bad behavior. These interpretations, while not denying the reality of suffering as a consequence of our spiritual ignorance and many errors, view Adam and Eve's eating the forbidden fruit as metaphor and/or as part of the divine plan. In other words, they view the fall as precisely what was supposed to happen because without falling into our human condition on Earth, the divine plan of evolution could not move forward. These views are obviously non-literal and tend to regard the Lord God's commanding Adam and Eve not to eat the forbidden fruit as a kind of divine ruse to accomplish God's intentions for creation and evolution. Two ongoing effects of God's ruse are that we possess some measure of free will and we do not enter human life knowing our true identity as children of God.

The purpose of the Lord God's ruse was to initiate, via human choice, the process of our evolution into separate-self consciousness apart from God and in relation to the resulting four Fruits of the Fall that define our human condition. It is in separate-self consciousness that we become aware of death/change, sex/desire, good/evil choices and our existential aloneness/incompleteness apart from God. Without the fall, we could have neither separation from God nor awareness of the four defining fruits together with the challenges and opportunities of contending with our limitations, allowing us to learn, choose, and grow through human ground into spiritual ground.

Existential parameter four, our aloneness/incompleteness apart from God, is the chief Fruit of the Fall. This fruit is the subtlest one, and it's what gives reality and power to the other three (allows us to perceive them). Hence it is the resolution of this fruit that ultimately frees us completely, resolving the basic problems of spiritual ignorance and uncertainty posed by human existence and depriving the other three fruits of their power to dominate, intimidate, and bewilder us.

Aloneness/incompleteness is at the root of our dualistic separate-self sense, which we need in order to perceive the opposites in created reality and thus to distinguish one thing from another. We need this dualistic perspective to function and survive in the world of human ground. Hence, our human ground programs us with a self/other orientation to created reality that, when taken to be absolute, becomes a ruse of false identity that stands in direct opposition to the inner perspective of our unifying, integrating spiritual ground. The dualistic separation of our learned identity in human ground creates division within us and gives rise to a profound sense of inner lack or a hole in our soul.

# 3

## HOLE IN THE SOUL AND SEX/DESIRE

I

When taken as a basis of who and what we are, our separate-self sense and experience of aloneness/incompleteness tell us that something essential (we know not what) is missing in us and our life. Our profound sense of something essential missing is experienced as a kind of hole in the soul. A haunting feeling of lack deep in our energy-field causes us to feel spiritually impoverished, hungry and in desperate need of something to fill the hole in, so we may feel content, whole and at peace. For example, when any of our basic instinctual needs are unmet, or perceived as unmet, we experience the uneasiness and pain of our hole in the soul, which is another name for the haunting Lost Paradise Archetype. What we most deeply need and desire on emotional and spiritual levels is felt to be lacking.

Until we come to know what we truly need and desire on the deepest level, we are bound to remain haunted and pained by our hole in the soul, pursuing happiness in places where it can't be found. As we pursue fulfillment in a state of spiritual ignorance, the elusive something we are seeking amid the bewildering Fruits of the Fall becomes for us whatever we believe will make us happy. We tend to identify unconsciously what we want with the Lost Paradise Archetype in our soul. Without consciously realizing it, we actually pursue something of this goal in all we desire, feeling compelled to find something to fill in our soul's aching hole. The urgency of this blind quest is the powerful motivation underlying the fruit of sex/desire rising from human ground and hidden deep in our soul.

The intense, unrelenting yearning created by our hole in the soul is the basis of our desire nature. We may try the pursuit of various attractions or programs for happiness, searching for what's needed to fill in our soul's inner hole. Though we may not realize or even dimly suspect it, this intense longing and need is ultimately the longing of the Serpent, or life force, within us, seeking return to Paradise via our evolution into divine union. It is the longing of our emotional desire nature that motivates us to action from beginning to end. The motivating force of our desire works through the compelling call of our basic instinctual needs and their various expressions in us.

When Adam and Eve were made to leave Paradise, the Serpent by the Tree of the Knowledge of Good and Evil went with them and, as evolutionary life force, became an essential, integral part of human nature. The "dust" this Serpent crawls in is our human ground. The Serpent lives within us as our instinctual desire nature and as the great longing for love to fill in our hole in the soul. The pursuit of various desires creates drama and stress in everyone's life, leading us through experiences of enjoyment, suffering, comedy, and tragedy.

At some point, we begin to understand that our desires and our needs are not always the same. As lower needs are met, higher needs of the soul awaken. As some desires are outgrown, new ones beckon us onward. Eventually, we discover our soul's spiritual longing for what we most truly need and desire (Paradise Found). This deepest longing is our need to reconnect with spiritual ground in the divine qualities and values of eternal love, truth, and freedom. That's what ultimately drives us, powering the Serpent of evolutionary life-force energy within us.

## II

To grasp the hole in our soul and the fruit of sex/desire, we need to understand the context in which we consciously perceive and experience them and their effects in us. This is the context of our separate-self sense and consciousness, which corresponds to the fourth Fruit of the Fall, our existential aloneness/incompleteness apart from God. Our separate-self sense, together with its transcendence into progressively higher, more integrated states of conscious wholeness, is central to the evolutionary theory of human spiritual development. Can this view, which leads beyond containment within dualistic categories of opposites, be reconciled with more traditional literal/tragic interpretations of the biblical Adam and Eve fall-from-paradise story? I believe it can be if we consider the following:

On the one hand, the painful tragedies of human suffering and the haunting dilemma of our inner aloneness/incompleteness in separation from the divine are obviously present and predominant in the human condition, as literal/tragic interpretations of the fall correctly tell us. On the other hand, as we learn through experience, the suffering and tragedy of our human condition are more than mere punishment for our wrongdoing. Many of our human pains, suffering and tragedies, especially those we unwittingly create ourselves, have a higher meaning and purpose for the soul related to our moral/ethical development, consciousness evolution and spiritual awakening, as evolutionary interpretations of the fall encouragingly tell us. With some reflection from this integral perspective, we may see the mutual complementarity of the tragic/literal and evolutionary interpretations.

So each view has something important to tell us and each is correct in its own light. Consequently, literal/tragic and evolutionary perspectives may be seen as mutually complementary rather than mutually exclusive, if we're willing to broaden our perspective into seeing the truth in each view and willing to be flexible and creative in our interpretations. To learn and grow spiritually always involves coming to see things in new ways.

A key question to ask in comparing tragic and evolutionary interpretations of the fall is, "At what point can we assume the existence of ego in Adam and Eve as a kind of absolute separate-self consciousness?" This is an important point of distinction typically overlooked by literal/tragic interpretations, which seem to assume Adam and Eve were created fully formed, both physically and psychologically, with full ego-consciousness and identity from the beginning. An evolutionary perspective, on the other hand, holds that the kind of ego-consciousness and identity we take for granted are products of humanity's historical, cultural, and psychological development over the course of many thousands if not millions of years. To integrate and reconcile literal/tragic interpretations of the fall with evolutionary interpretations, we need to assume the perspective of the evolution of ego-consciousness as developing from relative unconsciousness in living organisms on Earth. When Adam and Eve's "eyes were opened" in the biblical myth, they moved from a state of unknowing innocence into a new state of separate-self, ego-consciousness.

So what is meant by "ego," in terms of consciousness and identity? By ego, I mean: 1) a separating consciousness that distinguishes one thing from another, and 2) the eventual development of an assumed sense of separate-self identity based on the self-other perceptions of ego-consciousness. In our present human condition, we generally regard the perspective of ego as the given basis of reality and our perceptions of reality. Moreover, we tend to do this quite automatically or unconsciously, without questioning the validity of the assumption upon which ego is based; that is, the assumption of duality as the ultimate governing structure or principle of truth and reality. Ego-identity is the solidification of our separate-self sense into a fixed reference point within the changing field and perceptions of ego-consciousness.

From an evolutionary perspective, absolute ego-identity was clearly not present in Adam and Eve from the beginning. It did not become fully present in them until after the fall when they experienced the full force of existential parameter four, the fruit of our aloneness/incompleteness apart from God. The sense of real separation from the Lord God begins in the story when the Serpent suggests that they eat the forbidden fruit. The Serpent says, "You will not die; for God knows that when you eat of it your eyes will be opened, and you will be like God, knowing good and evil" (Genesis 3:4–5).

Adam and Eve's separation away from the Lord God begins there because this is the point where they are led to consider doing something contrary to what they believe the Lord God wants them to do. To go against the will of another is to create a barrier of separation and probable disharmony between oneself and that other. Such disharmony is often experienced when adolescents are in the process of separating psychologically from their parents in order to become more autonomous and independent individuals. Adam and Eve's eating the forbidden fruit was very much like this, as this act of rebellion intensified their ego-consciousness and set them psychologically apart from the Lord God's will and intentions, or at least so they thought.

The Serpent's words, "…God knows that when you eat of it your eyes will be opened," may be read to imply that God already knew Adam and Eve would eat the forbidden fruit, as God may secretly have intended. In their innocent state, Adam and Eve had to possess some minimal degree of self-consciousness apart from the Lord God in order to have a conscious relationship with the Lord God, a kind of relative ego-consciousness. They possessed enough ego-consciousness to choose to eat the forbidden fruit.

This fateful choice and the change of consciousness it brought Adam and Eve (knowledge of good and evil) had dramatic consequences. It propelled them into the human condition, causing them (us) to lose their innocence, to become alienated from the Lord God and subject to the Fruits of the Fall. The most fundamental consequence was that their separate-self sense, their sense of conscious ego-identity, went from being relative to absolute. Thus, upon expulsion from Paradise, they lost conscious connection to the Lord God, who personifies creation's divine Source and inner Ground of Being (our spiritual ground). From the inner emptiness and incompleteness created by this loss of connection to the divine come the four Fruits of the Fall and the voracious controlling appetites of our basic instinctual needs and desire nature, i.e., our hole in the soul. What is this hole in the soul?

## III

The hole in the soul is essentially our incompleteness as unfinished human and spiritual beings evolving in created reality. It is the unrelenting call of the Lost Paradise Archetype within us. This inner hole is the eternal longing of the mythical Serpent that is created reality's evolutionary energy, impetus and driving force (love divided seeking reunion). It is the basis of our desire nature, the inspirational energy that motivates us to action in pursuit of sex/desire, i.e., our quest for freedom, happiness, and fulfillment.

Our hole in the soul may be conceived as an inner chasm of long-ing created by the duality of the Feminine and Masculine Principles within us longing for union (completion). On the level of conscious awareness, the hole in our soul manifests as 1) our separate-self sense and 2) as our need or challenge to resolve the issues of the human condition posed by the Fruits of the Fall.

The Serpent, as instinctual life-force energy and impetus for evo-lution, is an essential foundation of human nature whence all our instinctual drives and needs emerge into expression. As we've seen, in biblical myth, the Serpent provoked the fall by tempting Adam and Eve to eat the fruit of good/evil so that the drama and evolution of human nature and consciousness could begin. This drama and evolu-tion carry with them the cost of conflict and suffering under the four Fruits of the Fall. The primal force of sex/desire, born of the Serpent's life-force energy, is the basic motive power causing the entire process of created reality to move, both in us and throughout the universe.

As created reality moves, the positive and negative consequences of good/evil and death/change are inevitable for all created persons and things. We cannot hold on to anything in created reality indefi-nitely because everything in creation is subject to death/change. To thrive under these conditions, we need to learn to trust the pro-cess of death/change rather than fear it, since the inevitability of death/change is the way of Nature, the way of divine law and will in created reality. To trust death/change is to be willing to let go of our fixations and attachments to various cherished objects of sex/desire when the natural time comes for us to part with them. This is not always easy to do since the roots of our strongest attachments tend to be hidden in the unconscious. Yet the death of one condition or form is always followed by change and renewal into another, making death and rebirth a continual process of life.

Without sex/desire, symbolized in the dynamic interactions and energy exchanges of opposites, we would simply let go and relax, allowing ourselves to rest and sink into the transcendent peace and abyss of the present moment beyond time, space and creation. With-out the attractions and energy exchanges of complementary oppo-sites separated by duality (the universal Feminine and Masculine

Principles), there would be no movement of energy or creation of reality on any level of phenomenal existence. Hence, the Serpent of duality and the movements of energy between its complementary poles are absolute prerequisites for creation to happen. The demiurge motivating this wondrous process is what we are calling sex/desire, the universal force of attraction/repulsion leading via evolution through multiplicity into unity and the eventual awakening of human consciousness into divine consciousness in created reality.

So sex/desire is what energizes us to action in human ground. The force of sex/desire in us and the choices it inspires implicitly indicate that we wish to change something about how things are in the immediate moment, unless we can let go of sex/desire and not follow its urgings. This has important implications for our spiritual state of being in terms of whether we choose to do or to be in the present moment, i.e., to change something via action or to relax and rest content, penetrating more deeply into what is via non-action. Wisdom counsels us that there is a time to do and a time to be and that ultimately these two (Masculine and Feminine Principles) are one in God or non-created Reality. God is simultaneously and paradoxically all being and all doing because the divine consciousness of non-created Reality is always one with everything.

The character of the Lord God in the Garden of Eden myth is simply an act of the universal divine consciousness portraying the origin of our human condition through the actions of Adam, Eve, the Serpent and the fall. As already stated, the Fruits of the Fall are the four basic parameters of our existence. Death/change is inevitable in time and creation. Sex/desire motivates us to action. Good/evil choices give us free will to test and develop our character. In addition, our existential aloneness/incompleteness is the foundation of our yearning quest for happiness and ultimately for our spiritual journey to lasting fulfillment. The four Fruits of the Fall challenge and torment us, prodding us on until we find completion in the love, truth and freedom of our true self and life in God (Paradise Found).

# 4

## Good/Evil in Human Ground

### I

Who has not pondered the searching question, what is the meaning of life? This important question has many possible answers. Some answers are temporary and shallow while others are more permanent and profound. For each of us, the meaning of life comes from what we care about and put our precious time, energy and heart into, be it shallow or profound. Love, the highest value of preciousness, is the ultimate meaning of life. The practical issue for each of us here concerns whom or what it is that we love, care for and put our time, energy and heart into? What is really valued and counted as important in our life? The answers to these questions, whether sacred, secular or profane, are the answers to how and where each of us finds personal meaning in life or the lack of it.

How we pursue meaning and fulfillment is a major ongoing existential issue that concerns every human being. This question is intimately related to the issues of what we want and how we go about pursuing our desires. To understand truly the question of life's meaning and what we want, we need to understand the nature of good/evil choices, the third Fruit of the Fall. It's not enough to know simply what's available to us via sex/desire. To reach the depths where real meaning resides, we need to become conscious of our inner motivations and the concomitant dimension of good/evil choices.

We need to grasp the significance of good/evil choices because lasting value and meaning for our soul's enrichment may come only from the genuine good. Our moral/ethical choices color the inner quality of our character, shaping what we become in relation to others, ourselves and in relation to God. Good moral/ethical choices align us with the spiritual values of our deep inner self, strengthening our character in the peace, preciousness, pure energy and eternal values of non-created Reality. They bring us into conscious harmony and alignment with our spiritual ground.

Evil moral/ethical choices, on the other hand, corrupt and destroy the soul's integrity with weak, divisive energy divorced from the enduring foundation of non-created Reality. The low road of evil moral/ethical choices may offer quicker results in the short term, gratifying some of our separate-self's egocentric desires, but such choices give no enduring fulfillment or self-respect in the soul. It happens this way because evil moral/ethical choices oppose the divine eternal values of love, truth, and freedom. Living true to these divine qualities and values is the only reliable source of lasting fulfillment for the soul; that is, they are the only way to our permanent Paradise Found. Evil sabotages the soul. Thus, we need to understand the true nature of good and evil, so we may attain deep meaning by choosing freely between them.

Good and evil may be conceived and defined in various ways, depending on our state of moral/ethical knowledge, our philosophical perspective, and our stage of consciousness evolution. The most primitive ideas of good/evil correlate them to our likes and dislikes, to suffering/enjoyment, pleasure/pain and so forth. Such subjective interpretations equate good and evil with ego-gratification versus ego-frustration. These subjective standards are not necessarily wrong, but they are arbitrary and relative to individual preferences and cultural/religious conditioning. They may reflect the perspective and values of only one side of our soul, the separate-self, human-ground side from which we experience life and reality apart from our Source. In some cases, one person's "good" may be another's "evil." An extreme example of this is a suicide bomber who believes he or she is doing the will of God or Allah versus the views of her or his victims and others who disagree.

Though both good and evil are always experienced subjectively by individuals, an objective standard for understanding them is desirable.

One source of a semi-objective standard we all possess is our innate, intuitive sense of right and wrong, commonly referred to as our "conscience." True conscience (as opposed to false conscience) is the voice of divine guidance within us, if we can hear or feel it. We are always free to pay it heed or to ignore it. If we habitually listen to and follow the voice of our true inner conscience, it grows stronger in us, aligning us with our spiritual ground and divine center. On the other hand, if we habitually ignore or defy it, our conscience grows increasingly weak.

In extreme cases, some individuals or groups appear to be without a conscience. This is because the true voice of conscience in them has been prevented from developing in early life by extreme abuse or neglect, or because a partially developed healthy conscience has been stifled, misguided, betrayed or repressed into the unconscious. If we can hear its voice, our true conscience knows in advance the outcomes of whatever choices we consider and always distinguishes clearly between good and evil for us.

In addition to our subjective conscience, and for the purposes of this book, we need an objective, spiritual standard for good and evil. I suggest the following: that which gives love, truth and freedom to the soul is good; and that which deprives the soul of love, truth and freedom is evil. This standard or definition for good and evil reflects the eternal qualities and values of non-created Reality and is, I believe, a spiritually accurate, mature, and evolved rendering.

Another, complementary definition of good/evil may be given in terms of universal morality and consciousness evolution. The eternal qualities and values of divine love, truth, and freedom for all constitute the basis of universal morality on the spiritual level. The progressive growth and expression of these divine qualities and values in soul and society lead directly to the evolution of human consciousness into divine consciousness. In other words, human consciousness evolution leads to the progressive fulfillment of God's divine plan for all of creation and each of us. That which serves the divine plan is good and that which opposes it is evil. Hence, the contrary anti-values of hatred, lies, and slavery oppose the divine plan and serve the basic agenda of evil. This too gives us a good working definition for good/evil on the spiritual level. Given this definition, the practical question then becomes one of discerning what truly does serve the divine plan and what actually opposes it, for evil may appear in the guise of good and good may, in some cases, be misjudged as evil.

## II

Given its unsavory character and obvious undesirability, one may well ask, why is there evil at all? And, does evil have a purpose or function in the grand scheme of God's plan? Evil does serve a necessary function for our evolution and growth in created reality. It cannot, however, exist in non-created Reality because, as the negative moral/ethical spiritual principle of creation, evil is part of a relative pair of opposites in created reality (good/evil). Relative evil exists in relation to relative good. Absolute good definitely exists, as the qualities and values of non-created Reality, but there can be no such thing as absolute evil because, in approaching its absolute level, it is in the nature of evil ultimately to destroy itself, as shall be explained below.

Absolute good consists of the divine eternal qualities, values, and consciousness of non-created Reality (God). Since the divine consciousness of non-created Reality contains all of relative created reality within its absolute oneness, non-created Reality also contains relative good and evil within itself as essential aspects of the spiritual drama in created reality. This does not mean, however, that evil exists in the eternal, perfect, absolute presence and pure consciousness of non-created Reality as it is in eternity. Evil is a created thing and exists only in some of the relative time/space dimensions of created reality, such as our human ground.

There is and can be no evil in eternity because what is eternal and timeless is the absolute good of divine love, truth, and freedom abiding forever in the mysterious pure consciousness of God. As creation's negative moral/ethical spiritual principle, it is the nature of evil to subvert, ruin and destroy both the good and the evil things in creation (in that order). When turned or directed in on its self, as if to become absolutely or purely what it is, evil destroys itself by the power of its own negation. This is always the inevitable end of evil, as we shall see in explaining sadomasochism, the inner face of evil on the spiritual level of created reality.

Good says "Yes" to creation, life, and existence, and evil says "No" to them. Hence, good supports God's divine plan for creation and evil opposes it. This is the fundamental spiritual drama and issue of creation: as Shakespeare's character, Hamlet, famously put it, "To be or not to be, that is the question." To choose the way of good is to choose "to be," and to choose the way of evil is to choose "not to be." This question of "to be or not to be" is ultimately the basic existential question of the human condition, a question we all must answer, individually and collectively, again and again throughout our lives. Do we choose to affirm or negate life, creation and ourselves? Which shall we be consumed by, love or hate, good or evil?

There can be no real drama in creation without conflict. Conflict requires opposition and the use of relative free will, the capacity to choose between alternatives. It's in this light that we can begin to understand the necessary function of evil. Evil adds to the plot and makes life interesting. Good/evil choices and conflicts provide each of us with the relative free will we need for developing the qualities and powers of our soul in its major spiritual rite of passage. Confrontation and conflict with evil are necessary for our spiritual growth. In opposing evil tendencies in ourselves, our souls grow stronger in virtue and goodness. In this way, our soul's inner evolutionary rite of passage takes us from the naïve curiosity and innocence of early life, through the folly, struggles, and rebellion of childish and adolescent selfishness/immaturity, into the knowing wisdom and freedom of spiritual maturity. This spiritual rite of passage requires time, experience and many conflicts within us between good/evil choices.

Completing this rite of passage is essential for our soul to grow up spiritually, so we may become full conscious participants in the divine love, truth and freedom of non-created Reality, which is absolute goodness and our precious spiritual heritage (Paradise Found). What this conscious participation in the divine consciousness is or will be like, we cannot say or imagine. It's something absolutely wonderful and mysterious beyond words, and shall be revealed to us only as we experience it directly through God's grace in meditation, prayer and life, initially by progressive degrees and ultimately in its total fullness. As we are consumed by the absolute goodness of divine love, truth and freedom, we shall become divine love, truth and freedom in our being and consciousness. We cannot accurately or fully imagine what this ultimate fulfillment of our soul's spiritual evolution will be like.

What we may say, however, is that our ever-growing participation in the divine consciousness has to be far more than the primal orgasmic ecstasy, bliss and undifferentiated unity of life's pure springing fountains at the beginning of creation, which some mistake for the ultimate spiritual awakening.[1] This rapturous diffusive orgasmic experience is, rather, an initial spiritual awakening, revealing the ecstatic oneness and bliss of creation's origins. Compared to where God's divine plan is leading us, it is a much lesser good. This is an important point to grasp because, to make our best ultimate choices and fulfill our highest destiny, we need to understand that it is only by way of God's divine plan (which involves evolving through created reality) that the greatest good may be attained or received.

One basic way to grasp the difference between good and evil is to see them in relation to our greatest good and God's divine plan. As stated above, relative good is the positive evolutionary force in created reality supporting true spiritual values and the divine plan, and relative evil is the complementary yet conflicting negative, anti-evolutionary force working against true spiritual values and the divine plan. These two opposing forces stimulate, energize, and balance each other, and the conflicts between them generate tremendous creativity in our evolutionary process as well as much destruction and death. Evil serves as the necessary foil or counter-force for evolving creation, life, and consciousness.

As this process unfolds, good is present in all positive evolutionary expressions of death/change, and evil is there in all negative devolutionary expressions of death/change. In choosing ultimately "not to be," evil is opting for unconsciousness via the far lesser good of returning as quickly as possible to the blissful undifferentiated unity of orgasmic primal chaos preceding created reality's formation. In choosing fully "to be," on the other hand, good is opting for the greatest of goods to be attained by individual souls and all of creation. This is the noble, heroic choice of undertaking the long laborious evolutionary journey and struggle of consciousness and life in conflict with the inertia and resistance of evil through time, space, and substance. The eventual spiritual victory of this struggle is required for bringing God's divine plan into its completion, fruition, and fulfillment. Thus, good affirms phenomenal existence on all levels of creation (visible and invisible), and ultimately aspires to co-create with God in service of the divine plan.

## III

Both good and evil seek return to non-created Reality: good through the path of positive creation and God's divine plan, and evil by the negative regressive way of destruction, death, and unconsciousness. These two ways for the energy of created reality in us to return to non-created Reality are the spiritual basis of good/evil in human ground; that is, human nature is attracted to the ways of both good and evil. This inner conflict is present in all of us and is the basis of human free will on the moral/ethical level. In addition to their spiritual origins as ways of return to non-created Reality, good and evil in human ground also have historical, evolutionary roots related to the universal survival instinct in all terrestrial life forms.

We have inherited instinctual tendencies toward kindness and cruelty from our early evolutionary ancestors and other animal-kingdom life forms. Kindness comes from the nurturing of newborns and from the formation and loyalty of cooperative social units within various species. Cruelty comes from the predator-prey game of carnivorous survival and from brutal and sometimes deadly competition within and among various species. It is Nature's way that "life feeds upon life" in the waters, jungles, gardens, skies and deserts of terrestrial life forms. Pleasure is found in this activity to help keep the process of life going.

Life-form species in the animal kingdom are relatively innocent in their kindness and cruelty where moral/ethical issues of good/evil do not exist for them. Animals are compelled by instinct, and their consciousness has not evolved to the moral/ethical level of conscience as we know it. In human ground, we have inherited instinctual tendencies toward kindness and cruelty along with a sexual drive toward pleasure and reproduction from the animal kingdom. But in our human kingdom, as symbolized by Adam and Eve eating the forbidden fruit, we have the added responsibility of free will and good/evil choices. Consequently, what is relatively innocent cruel behavior in animals may become perverse and evil in humans, as, for example, in the sadomasochistic enjoyment of dominating, torturing and harming others or being a victim.

In sadomasochistic perversion, evil is done for its own sake, for the love of it as an end in itself. Complete sadomasochism is the final phase of human descent into evil where goodness is hated and consciously opposed. Such extremes are rare and sadomasochism, as a conscious orientation, is far down the road of succumbing to evil, far down the road of hatred, lies, and slavery. Before one reaches such a stage of deadly descent, there are a number of prior steps in the soul's moral/ethical corruption and perversion away from health and goodness, unless an individual comes out of a toxic environment where cruelty and abuse are a way of life.

Loving formative experiences of nurturing and bonding to parents are crucial to the foundation of our moral/ethical character in human ground. When our early-life needs are met and our goodness affirmed, then it becomes natural and easy to affirm the needs, rights, and worth of others as we grow into adults. As goodness grows in us, we come to care more and more for the needs, wellbeing, and rights of others, and for the quality of health and life throughout our world—which extends to all people and species of life forms on our planet and beyond.

Goodness grows in a heart of peace, compassion, and kindness. Such a heart opposes evil, not by force of resistance but by transcending separations of duality through an empathic inner vision of unity and shared identity. Evil requires separation and absolute ego-identity apart from its target or master. Goodness, on the other hand, bridges all gaps of separation and egocentric illusion via the altruistic caring of inner relatedness and shared identity in the love and oneness of spiritual ground. We may rise to this spontaneous inner vision of goodness and caring only by growing through the relative factual illusions of our ego-consciousness and identity in human ground. It is a participation in the consciousness of our true self and Paradise Found.

Good and evil grow in us with the desires and habits of thought, feeling and action that form our character. The quality of meaning in each person's life correlates to the quality of what or whom he or she wants and truly cares about; and the spiritual core of our character in human ground is formed by what we desire and care about as well as by how we go about pursuing our desires. Is it good or evil, cruelty or kindness, cheating or playing fair? The inner conflict between the desires of our false self versus those of our true self occupies center stage in this high stakes competition between good and evil in our soul.

IV

The progressive stages of descent into the ways of evil begin from where most of us are; that is, in a state of mixed motivations involving the conflicting desires and agendas of our false self and our true self. For those of us who are consciously striving to direct our lives toward growth in goodness and service to God, the motivations of our false self tend to undercut our well-intentioned efforts and to remain hidden in the unconscious. Unawareness of our false self's activities within us can keep us stuck in our spiritual journey for a long time, especially if we're unwilling to consciously admit this and the reality of what's going on within us.

The second stage of descent into evil involves consciously making moral/ethical compromises to get something our false self wants. For example, we may mislead or manipulate others by telling a little lie or not all of the truth. This is not done because we want to do it or enjoy doing it, but because we feel it's necessary to achieve some desired outcome. We may rationalize, excuse or try to cover up our moral/ethical compromise, telling our self it is really necessary, for the greater good and that "the end justifies the means." Since what we're doing is really self-centered, our justifications involve self-deceptions of lying to our self so we can feel okay about it. The deeper into evil we go, the greater our self-deceptions grow.

Next, it becomes a matter of frequency and degree. Do we do this just once and continue to cover it up? Do we confess it and repent? Or do we continue in this kind of behavior, possibly moving on to more serious violations of conscience and moral/ethical standards? If we continue down the road of self-deception and moral/ethical decline, the third stage of descent into evil is reached as we come to associate lying, stealing, cheating, or whatever with getting what we want. It becomes a pattern in our character that may develop into a pathological criminal mind. A lot of energy is spent in justifying and covering up what we're doing, and all of this energy serves to feed and strengthen our false self while suppressing our conscience. This is dangerous territory.

There may be some conscious warning signs but the harm occurring in our soul is mostly kept hidden in the unconscious. Various ego-fantasies of self-delusion shield our conscious awareness from the ugly truth of what's going on inside us. Just as love, truth and freedom for the soul are the natural results of practicing goodness; so are hate, lies, and slavery inevitable consequences of following the path of evil. We may travel a long way down evil's path before grasping this truth and learning evil's sad lessons, one of which is that lying makes us stupid.

The fourth stage of descent into evil is reached as manipulating, harming and deceiving others becomes for us an art and game we play with relish and delight, rather than reluctantly or with regret. As we begin to enjoy the drama, excitement and power of doing evil, it becomes not only a means to getting things we want but an end in itself that gives us amusement and pleasure. This involves the deliberate forsaking and betrayal of our conscience in favor of its adversary.

Doing evil for its own sake, for the wicked thrills, power and enjoyment of it, is the path to addiction to evil. This point marks a threshold, beyond which lies the willful perversion of conscience and unrestrained degradation of our character. Here, there's little reason to cover up our duplicity and transgressions for the sake of our conscience. The only covering up we'd do would be to deceive and mislead others, which requires effective acting skills.

The lure and enjoyment of evil as an end in itself, whether chosen consciously or not, include taking pleasure in causing harm to others and seeing them suffer. This is an entry point into sadomasochistic perversion, which is the inner face of evil. The seeds of sadomasochism exist in every human soul, as do our divine potentials as spiritual beings. Sadomasochism generally remains unconscious and may hide behind the masks of all conceivable roles and under the appearance of every possible disguise in life's drama.

Like all forms of evil, sadomasochism requires the illusion of absolute separate-self identity in order to act out its perverse fantasies. It is a two-sided equation consisting of active sadism and passive masochism. Sadists enjoy dominating and giving pain to others as well as watching others suffer. Masochists enjoy creating self-sabotage to bring domination, pain and suffering to oneself. Like all pairs of complementary opposites, sadism and masochism depend on each other and form a polar unity. Consequently, inside every sadist there's a masochist and inside every masochist a sadist. When one side of this perverse polarity is conscious, its polar opposite remains unconscious and is unconsciously projected onto the sadomasochist's partner in some sadomasochistic ego-fantasy. Sadomasochists unconsciously identify with their victims/abusers, thereby experiencing a kind of pseudo-intimacy, self-transcendence and secret oneness with them. This is the ultimate perversion of our deep need for intimacy/belonging.

Sadomasochism is the offspring of evil's terrestrial and spiritual roots in the human soul; that is, it's the progeny of our inherited instinctual tendency toward cruelty combined with the impetus to return to non-created Reality by negating life and creation via destruction. This is a recipe fueled by hatred and rage. In sadomasochism lies the secret paradox of evil, which consists in hating and loving at the same time. It's like hating to love and loving to hate, reveling in a contradiction of seductive cross-purposes, surrendering and losing one's self while falling helplessly into a hellish holocaust abyss of hatred and evil.

Pain and pleasure become one in the perverse delights of sadomasochism. They become one on the horrible, obscene, exciting, and ruinous road to separate-self disintegration and death via hatred, lies and slavery. Saying "yes" to "no" and "no" to "yes" are the essence of sadomasochism. This is the inner face of evil. It is the tragic face of creation's archetypal Serpent choosing "not to be" by bitterly biting and eating its own twisted tail.

## V

To encourage the continuation of any behavior pattern, those practicing it need to find it enjoyable or rewarding in some way. Hence, evil begins to win out as it becomes an enjoyable end in itself for its practitioners, as does good. Evil's hidden agenda is always our undoing, i.e., the negation of God's plan in us and in created reality. This is because the inner spiritual impetus and ultimate goal of evil is to return to non-created Reality by way of our destruction, both individually and collectively. Cruelty and enjoyment of sadomasochistic perversions lend themselves well to this agenda, as do all forms of hatred, lies, and slavery that say "no" to life and to the higher spiritual values of love, truth and freedom for all.

The love of goodness leads to integration and wholeness of soul. The love of evil brings us ultimately to psychotic disintegration and the abyss of death. Goodness begets goodness and evil begets more evil. It's not just what's in the living room of our conscious awareness that we have to contend with, but what's hidden underground in the root cellar of our unconscious motivations and desires. The primal conflict between good and evil underlies the inner opposition between true self and false self in every human soul. This and unconsciousness are what make overcoming evil and the obstacles of our false self so challenging and difficult. Fortunately, God lives in our soul and divine help is available from within, if we humbly ask and are willing to allow the inner work of our purification, healing and transformation to move forward.

As Thomas Keating teaches,[2] the unconscious foundational patterns of the conscious personality or separate-self sense (false self) need to be transformed by the divine indwelling before any lasting or meaningful change can take place within the human individual. This may happen only with our willing consent and cooperation; that is, our consent to the divine presence and action working in our soul and life, and our willingness to give up or let go of all patterns of thought, feeling and action that are contrary to God's will for us. If we are not willing to acknowledge and forsake our obstacles to spiritual growth, how will we ever get free of them?

# Part Two

# Our Basic Instinctual Needs and Happiness Programs

# 5

# Our Basic Needs, Part One

## Security / Survival / Safety

I

We cannot come to know ourselves in any deep way until we truly understand what we want, need and why. We are all born with certain basic instinctual needs and it is from these that our natural healthy desires and their perversions originate. Our basic instinctual needs are the hardwired motivational programming in human ground. This built-in motivational programming is part and parcel of our conscious and unconscious instinctual desire nature. The healthy satisfaction of our basic needs leads eventually to the awakening of our spiritual ground. However, our basic instinctual needs are rarely, if ever, fully satisfied or understood by any of us. We all tend to suffer various forms of wounding around our basic needs and this leads to retardation in our development as human beings and spiritual beings. It leads to confusion and misdirection of our desire-energy.

Our basic instinctual needs arise in human ground within the context of the four Fruits of the Fall. It is inevitable that we are to desire ardently what we truly require to live, grow and experience wellbeing in human life. The fire of desire is the engine that runs our soul. However, our fallen, wounded human condition being what it is, our desires may be either true or false to our real needs of body and soul. An essential part of acquiring wisdom lies in coming to know consciously what our true needs actually are, and being able to distinguish them from other desires that are counterfeit substitutes for what we truly need and want. Unfortunately, much of what we think we need or have learned to want is not what we really need at all.

The search for wisdom and spiritual growth in human ground is the drama of our quest for liberation from the immature, misguided desires of our false self, and for the discovery, fulfillment, and freedom of the real needs and desires of our true self. This universal quest of the human condition comes about as a consequence of the fall, as a result of having been wounded in various ways around our basic needs when we were innocent and helpless. Actually, our wounding is what ends our innocence.

Our basic instinctual needs have both material and spiritual roots of origin. The material, earthly roots of our basic needs may be seen in the long process of terrestrial evolution. Our human ground is largely but not completely a product of this evolution, since we share our most basic physical and emotional needs with other, less evolved species of life forms. The most fundamental of these needs is that for self-preservation, commonly called "the survival instinct" or "will to live."

The presence and action of will imply directionality, intentionality, or purpose within life and creation. It implies the presence of some innate unconscious desire or, in higher evolved life forms, some conscious longing to move in a particular direction. The end goal of created reality's evolution comes from the spiritual roots of our basic needs. In the long course of evolution on Earth, we can see the progressive unfolding of four kingdoms in Nature: the mineral, vegetable, animal and human kingdoms. And we may intuit the presence of an unseen fifth "spiritual kingdom" into which terrestrial life and consciousness are evolving.

That this wondrous process is much more than the result of random chance and blind accident is obvious, if we consider the intricate patterns of energy-flow, form, change, and the meticulous organization of Natural Law that bring it about.[1] There is clearly some underlying principle of intelligent organization, design, or purpose behind and within the natural process of created reality as manifested in the physical universe and beyond. Something is intentionally causing it all to happen and work as it does. There is a conscious organizing principle or Source outside of creation that is manifesting the universe of created reality within its non-created consciousness. We may call this conscious organizing principle "God," "non-created Reality," or whatever we like. It is what it is and we live and exist within it.

This something or God is what we are calling our "spiritual ground." It is the omnipresent center of all centers, the universal heart of all hearts, the inner holy ground from which all created reality is issuing forth into manifestation. We may also refer to this sustaining inner ground and its workings as "the divine plan." Actually, the divine plan of creation is the ongoing manifestation of non-created Reality in created reality, equivalent to the Laws of Nature both physical and spiritual. In other words, Nature's Laws and the divine plan are expressions of the divine will that is the Source of all being and becoming in created reality. The central point here is that the ultimate Source of both terrestrial evolution and the instincts of evolving life is the holy ground and divine will of non-created Reality. Hence, the ultimate Source of our human ground is our spiritual ground. In Reality, we are never apart from our spiritual ground though, through much of life's evolution, God's spiritual ground is hidden from our sight.

In the animal kingdom, created reality's evolving life force becomes mobile, entering into new complexities of awareness, behavior, relationship, and experience beyond those of the plant kingdom. The basic survival instinct, first observable in the plant kingdom, now evolves into a variety of new instinctual activities and relationships, including eating, drinking, hunting, courting, mating, nurturing offspring and the famous "fight or flight" response. Along with these activities and the relationships around them, new experiences and manifestations of the root survival instinct come into expression. These include emotional consciousness and the formation of relationships, competitions, rivalries, cooperative social groups and the creation of power hierarchies within those groups. Cooperation becomes a key to survival as couples and groups band together for mutual benefit, support and to pursue common instinctual goals of species reproduction and continuity.

In animal emotions, behavior and consciousness, we see the evolutionary precursors of human emotions, behavior and consciousness. These include mutual caring and raising offspring (kindness), and the beginnings of sadomasochism (cruelty) in mating rituals and the archetypal predator/prey game initiated by carnivorous animals. The survival instinct in animals has evolved beyond the physical necessities of survival into rudimentary appetites and needs for sensation/pleasure, affection/caring, dominance/submission, power/control and group identification.

As human beings and spiritual beings, we have basic instinctual needs for security/survival/safety, sensation/pleasure, affection/esteem/approval, power/control and intimacy/belonging. As our lower needs for survival and wellbeing are met, our higher needs for spiritual growth begin to dawn in consciousness, unless we are distracted and held back by our false self. Due to the great power of our survival instinct, we are bound to remain compelled by worldly goals until our requirements for living in the world are met. Once we have what we legitimately need to live in the world, we may then learn to become "in the world but not of it" by seeing beyond what the world has to offer into the far greater goods, higher values and inner-wealth treasure of our spiritual ground. The false self, however, which persistently denies that our lower needs have been met, even when they are met, will tend to keep us fixated on worldly goals far beyond our attaining what we legitimately need to live and function in the world. One of the chief limitations of the false self is its inveterate spiritual blindness and concomitant fixation on isolated separate-self identity.

The divine origin of our human ground and its basic instinctual needs is our spiritual ground. Our spiritual ground is the source of the divine plan, which becomes conscious and active in us as we move into the higher stages of evolution. Our inner spiritual ground is the origin, inspiration and goal of created reality's directionality and ultimate purpose. We may live consciously in human ground and spiritual ground at the same time. However, at some point in our advancing evolution, our human ground will drop away and we shall come to live entirely in our spiritual ground, the fifth and most wonderful kingdom of Nature.

## II

The basic instinctual need for security/survival/safety is our fundamental existential need that extends into all levels of our life. This need is with us throughout life but changes dramatically over time in the ways we may experience and meet it. In early life, our physical and emotional needs related to security/survival/safety are of primary importance and we are totally dependent on others to meet these needs by giving us nourishment, protection, care, and support. As we grow up, developing power/control, we gradually learn to become less dependent on others and more self-reliant, learning that we can take action to get some of our needs met. As we become more conscious, where we look for security/survival/safety tends to change dramatically in relation to our other basic needs and the four Fruits of the Fall. That is, the kinds of security/survival/safety we seek tend to expand out into new areas.

When our need for security/survival/safety is adequately met, our foundation is firm and we are able to grow forward in human ground, experiencing life as good and change as enjoyable movement into new states of positive wellbeing. When our security/survival/safety need is not adequately met, our growth is stunted and we tend to experience life as unstable and uncertain. Change then tends to be experienced as questionable and ominous, threatening us with uncertainty and possible suffering via privation of our wants and needs.

In early life, we must rely on our parents or caretakers to meet our needs for security/survival/safety on the physical and emotional levels. We are dependent on our parents to give us affirmation, support, and encouragement, and to teach and guide us into the world where we must live and survive. Our basic physical needs for clean air and pure water, for healthy food and shelter, for protection from danger, for clothing, exercise, and rest, are the material foundation of our need for security/survival/safety. Our basic instinctual need for affection/esteem/approval is the emotional basis of our need for security/survival/safety. If these needs are not met to some minimal degree, we will fall ill under the specter of death/change, suffer, and die. Hence, we all owe a tremendous debt of gratitude to those (like our parents) who have loved and provided for us what we could not provide for ourselves, and who have nourished, protected and helped us to meet our basic needs for physical and emotional security/survival/safety.

Beyond its physical and emotional requirements, our basic instinctual need for security/survival/safety has vital, mental, psychic, social, and spiritual components. Thus, our basic instinctual needs for sensation/pleasure, power/control and intimacy/belonging all contain within them certain essential elements of our core existential need for security/survival/safety. This is because we need security/survival/safety on every level of our being, every level on which we exist. In fact, though each of our instinctual needs has clearly developed into an essential basic need in its own right, all our basic needs may be seen as extensions or further evolutions of the original security/survival/safety need. Our primordial survival instinct extends into all areas of human activity, relationship, and experience. Thus, security/survival/safety is like the trunk of a tree with our other basic needs as its branches, flowers, and fruit.

Security/survival/safety is supported by our basic instinctual need for sensation/pleasure. Positive sensation/pleasure involves life's many enjoyments, including feelings of wellbeing and happiness. Whenever any basic instinctual need is met, we enjoy positive experiences of sensation/pleasure. These sensate experiences, which may be physical, vital, emotional, mental, and so on, tell us that life is good and their enjoyment inspires us to want more of life; thus reinforcing our desire and need for security/survival/safety. We come to associate experiencing various forms of positive sensation/pleasure with feeling safe, secure, and enjoyably alive.

Power/control is essentially our need for personal independence and freedom in human ground. Power/control plays a key role in allowing us to meet our need for security/survival/safety, as well as all our other basic instinctual needs. The healthy fulfillment of our need for power/control is many-faceted. It includes the various abilities and skills we learn and develop in all areas of life, our belief system and sense of orientation to reality, and our ability to make intelligent decisions in harmony with healthy conscience. Power/control thus obviously helps us to meet our core existential need for security/survival/safety on all levels.

Our need for intimacy/belonging is both a social and a spiritual need. It is both an outer need in relation to others and an inner need in relation to our self and God. Our existential need for security/survival/safety extends into both our outer life in society and our inner life. That is, we need to feel safe, secure and to survive in our relationships to others and in relation to our self and God. Healthy human relationships, the self-respect that comes from living true to our conscience and intimacy in our relationship with God all contribute to this.

All we experience in human ground is obviously temporary, passing and subject to the fruit of death/change. Our relationship to God, on the other hand, is an eternal relationship that transcends death/change and the other Fruits of the Fall: sex/desirer, good/evil choices, and our aloneness/incompleteness apart from God. Hence, our soul's final refuge is in our eternal relationship to God.

## III

The ultimate fulfillment of our existential need for security/survival/safety may be realized only through our need for intimacy/belonging in relation to God. All our other relationships are temporary and subject to death/change. Ultimate refuge in the divine is something promised and spoken of in the world's religious and spiritual traditions as an antidote to our fears of uncertainty and death. Whether it's eternal reward or punishment in heaven or hell, a paradise of ideal pleasure, union with God, enlightenment or participation in the inner worlds of spiritual hierarchies in service of God's divine plan, all traditions extol the purpose and goal of our spiritual awakening and participation in the higher designs of the One Divine Consciousness.

Our existential emergence from human ground into spiritual ground is a movement from subjection to the Fruits of the Fall and our basic instinctual needs into the final freedom and fulfillment of our fundamental need for security/survival/safety. Hearing of such a marvelous possibility, we may well ask, "What could it be like?"

Various answers to this question have been given throughout human history in the myths, legends, and scriptures of the world's cultures and religions, and also by speculative philosophers and theologians. To conclude this chapter's discussion of our basic instinctual need for security/survival/safety, I'd like to share a few answers to the question of its ultimate fulfillment:

There is inside us, in the deepest center of our being, an integral depth-consciousness that unites the universe of created reality with the ineffable pure consciousness of non-created Reality or God. This is where the essence of our human ground joins the heart of our spiritual ground beyond time and space in the golden place of love's eternal treasure (Paradise Found). This is the place of our ultimate security/survival/safety where nothing may threaten or harm us.

The movement of creation's life-force energy from duality into love's oneness happens through the evolution of consciousness from human ground into spiritual ground. When our true self fully awakens, our awareness is said to become a focal point of individual consciousness resting in its true center and radiating out the universal qualities, fullness, and values of non-created Reality.[2] Such an individual consciousness, which is both unique and universal, becomes a house of heart's treasure overflowing goodness and fulfillment of all desires. What could this be like?

We might imagine our soul's Paradise Found to be something like what Jungian Psychologist Robert A. Johnson calls "the golden world."[3] In that golden inner world of dynamic wholeness, all opposites are united and completed in one another. When separated in the realm of duality, they long for one another to join and become complete in the holy magic of heart's treasure to find. This hunger and yearning for wholeness is the hole in our soul, the gap in our gaze from time toward eternity, the vision of our longing to join in love's embrace where life's truth, beauty and goodness fill up the cup of our soul, sublime and divine in the pure energy of oneness, immortality, perfection. Our soul's Paradise Found is an inconceivable fullness of inner wealth welling up inside us, a shining sun of living liquid gold radiating preciousness throughout the soul, overflowing its holding cup with infinite happiness, peace and love for all. It is a loving union of serenity and bliss, the legendary Philosopher's Stone of immortal wisdom harvested in the soul from life's pure springing fountains.

The Buddha, when asked to describe the essence of his teaching, is reported to have silently held up a flower. On another occasion, the Buddha was asked about the consciousness of supreme Enlightenment and said that this state is inconceivable to the human intellect or imagination. He then went on to compare it to something like a timeless, shoreless ocean of divine immortal light containing an infinite net of wish-fulfilling jewels (individual souls or energy-fields), each reflecting the entire ocean and all its jewels within itself in perfect love, harmony and pure consciousness.[4] The Buddha's living net of individual consciousness-jewels perhaps equates to the Christian idea of the communion of saints in the mystical Body of Christ whose lamp universal is love eternal and inconceivable, known only by entering in to conscious participation via divine grace and direct experience.

This vision of integral wholeness uniting the unique and the universal in the individual soul's divine spiritual ground suggests the ultimate fulfillment of our soul's need for security/survival/safety (Paradise Found). Such unimaginable fulfillment is perhaps equivalent to what Christ's "kingdom of heaven" may be as a fully conscious state of spiritual completion and maturity for the individual soul in union with God and all souls. This vision of the "New Jerusalem" or "kingdom of heaven" seems much more likely and real to me than the idea of heaven being some form of immortality for the separate-self ego or a paradise for our self-centered false self. In any case, final resolution to our core need for security/survival/safety, and to the four Fruits of the Fall, will come only through the fulfillment of our deepest spiritual need for intimacy/belonging in relation to God and the spiritual ground of our being. It is so because this alone is our true and ultimate security/survival/safety originated and awaiting us in the boundless eternity of now.

# 6

# Our Basic Needs, Part Two

## Sensation / Pleasure, Affection / Esteem / Approval

I

Our need for sensation/pleasure lets us know we are alive. It is our need to discover the world, experience our aliveness and to enjoy life. The various sensations we experience from within and without stimulate us to respond and thereby bring us to consciousness in life. The pleasures we enjoy serve to affirm life's beauty and goodness. The sensations we experience are like a symphony of ever-changing positive and negative impressions through which we contact our world. The pleasures they may bring are like a rainbow of harmony and promise, telling us life is good and will keep getting better, if we learn the art of enjoyment and don't get stuck on one level of pleasure through attachment, greed, addiction, or overindulgence.

The basic bent of consciousness is movement toward increasing pleasure, enjoyment, delight, satisfaction, rapture, ecstasy, and bliss. It is a movement through human ground leading ultimately to divine union in spiritual ground. We are naturally motivated toward delight, gravitate to enjoyment, and are attracted by what feels good. We are made to seek and discover differing degrees of pleasure involving sensations on different levels of our being, ranging from the physical to the spiritual. The progressive refinement of our pleasures leads us through human experience into the higher qualities of consciousness and caring in our spiritual ground.

Getting our needs met always gives us wonderful sensation/pleasure. All we experience in life stimulates our consciousness in human ground and beyond. Our basic need for sensation/pleasure is our need for fun, excitement, drama, adventure, and laughter. Much of this comes to us in connection with other people. The pleasures we experience affirm life's rich goodness, telling us life's a precious gift meant to be enjoyed.

As sensations/pleasures come and go, they express the fruit of death/change in their impermanence. They are like steps in a dance that keeps on moving. We cannot hold on to them, keep, freeze, or possess them. If we try they die and we lose their magic and our place in the dance. The dance goes on with or without us. All sensations/pleasures are fleeting movements in time vanishing like echoes of a sound gone by. They come and go like water flowing down a stream, pointing beyond their passing existence into an elusive something beyond yet within this ephemeral world.

They point to mystery's timeless Source, to the eternal promise of our spiritual ground. Appreciation, reverence, and gratitude for the beauty and wonder of life's pleasures are doors to our participation in an abiding goodness that does not pass like water running down a stream. As we learn to let passing sensations/pleasures come and go, without grasping or trying to possess, we become free to enjoy them fully and to pass pleasantly through them. We become free to stay present now where the moment opens to reveal the next step in life's ongoing dance. This is the subtle art of pleasure: passing through and beyond life's momentary sensations to enter into conscious participation in the timeless dimension of creation's ground of being unfolding hidden secrets of our true home and divine inner Source.

Our need for sensation/pleasure invites us to experience the celebration of life on all levels, from the material to the spiritual. Our physical senses are the entry level for experiences of sensation/pleasure. Here we encounter a wide range of gross contacts and subtle refinements bringing us sharply and intently into life in the present moment. Beyond the physical level, we encounter an even more complex array of psychological sensations/pleasures, including our responses to various physical stimuli, emotions, thoughts, and intuitions. The energy exchanges of human interactions and relationships provide us with many more possibilities of sensation/pleasure, ranging from the dramatic to the intimate, from comedy to tragedy, and from the entertaining to the enlightening. The art of pleasure is an art of embracing and releasing, an art of encountering fully, nakedly and openly, and freely letting go.

The higher forms of sensation/pleasure are spiritual and involve the stimulation of our energy-field by higher, more universal frequencies of consciousness-energy vibrations emanating from spiritual ground. Such experiences may be attributed to the action of divine grace, may occur at any time but most often happen when we forget our self in the moment, or are deep in prayer or meditation. Such sublime sensation/pleasure experiences, which are deeply subjective and personal, may also involve contact with higher evolved non-physical spiritual guides and teachers. Our soul's multidimensional capacities for interactions and relationships range from our visible human ground into our invisible spiritual ground.

Beyond the various experiences of sensation/pleasure encountered in human ground, the hidden jewel of light, life, and love, shining in the center of our soul is our deeper consciousness in spiritual ground. The profound peace, contentment, ecstasy, and bliss of sacred presence revealed within us gradually become our participation in the subtler refinements of spiritual ground manifesting in consciousness. Such graced transient experiences go beyond human ground and become the ultimate fulfillment of our need for sensation/pleasure.

In the process of moving through human ground into spiritual ground, we experience various gradations of sensation/pleasure on all levels of our being. Our physical, vital, emotional, mental, psychic, social, and spiritual dimensions become united in spiritual ground. Through all of this, our basic instinctual need for sensation/pleasure interacts with the Fruits of the Fall. That is, death/change, sex/desire, good/evil choices and our aloneness/incompleteness apart from God all interact with our basic need for sensation/pleasure.

Death/change is continually present in the sensations of all pleasures as well as pains, since these phenomena are temporary and cause changes in us. The fruit of sex/desire likewise relates to sensation/pleasure in that we are naturally inclined to want and pursue what feels good and to avoid what is unpleasant. The pursuit of more and more sensation/pleasure expresses our appetite for life and its enjoyment. To fulfill this longing best, we need to learn the art of pleasure in the dance of sex/desire, which calls for a delicate balance between involvement and detachment, indulgence and restraint.

Just as good food tastes best when we're hungry, the contrasts between opposites create intensity of experience in all our enjoyments of sensation/pleasure. Overindulgence inevitably dulls our sensitivity and ability to enjoy; hence our need of moderation and self-restraint in all pleasures. With simple presence and mindfulness, all of life's pleasures may be made to yield their treasures, when we know how to use them as stepping-stones to spiritual ground.

Moral/ethical considerations of good/evil choices are often involved regarding how we treat others and our self in pursuing the sensations/pleasures we desire. Issues of good/evil choices confront us in terms of both what we enjoy and how we go about pursuing it. For example, the healthy enjoyment of life's natural pleasures is good and life affirming, while abuse and overindulgence in legitimate pleasures as well as various unhealthy pleasures are evil and ultimately life-negating. While good celebrates the beauty and delight of all healthy pleasures, evil, if not overindulgent, abusive, or perverse, tends to condemn many if not all legitimate pleasures as selfish and sinful. These two contrary attitudes of evil toward pleasure (the positive/overindulgent/abusive attitude and the negative/rejecting/judgmental attitude) express evil's inherently sadomasochistic nature, which, in either case, seeks to sabotage life's goodness and our healthy enjoyment of it. The path of health and sanity is the middle way of balance and moderation between extremes of indulgence, judgment, and restraint.

The stimulation created by various experiences of sensation/pleasure usually tends to distract us from encountering the fourth Fruit of the Fall, our existential aloneness/incompleteness apart from God. In addition to this, as mentioned above, certain healthy experiences of sensation/pleasure may serve to bring us into conscious contact with our spiritual ground. This becomes especially true in our grateful appreciation of life's beauty and goodness when we go through fleeting sensation/pleasure into the present moment's timeless dimension.

On the other hand, too little sensation/pleasure or boredom with it caused by overindulgence, mechanical repetition or abuse, tends to confront us with our aloneness/incompleteness as whatever we're doing or not doing becomes empty, meaningless and unsatisfying. This is a common consequence of prudish repression, overindulgence, and habituation to self-centered, greedy attitudes toward sensation/pleasure. Discovering simple appreciation and openness to what's happening now, without grasping or rejecting, frees us from the unhealthy approaches of overindulgence, abuse, and prudish avoidance.

Sensation/pleasure invites us to embrace life-experience. Whenever we experience any pleasure, there's always a climactic point where our enjoyment reaches its height of intensity and we partly lose our separate-self to become one with the experience. This may be so subtle and slight that we scarcely notice it; or it may be almost overwhelming as we are lost and absorbed into the experience. All experiences of sensation/pleasure have a crescendo point, which I call "pleasure's peak." It's their limit or high point. This crescendo moment is a point of oneness, like the peak of a wave where all its energy crests. It's the point where we may merge into the now-moment, going beyond the sensation/pleasure we're experiencing by relaxing into and passing through it. Such open entry into pleasure's peak and release into the now-moment reveal the high art of true pleasure where having and letting-go are one.

## II

Our basic instinctual need for affection/esteem/approval is essentially our need for emotional security, reassurance, support, and positive self-regard. In other words, it's our need to feel accepted, to like, and to feel good about our self. The giving and receiving of affection/esteem/approval in human relationships grows out of our instinctual tendency toward kindness and the nurturing of growth and wellbeing in self and others. On the other hand, the denial or abuse of this need hurts us emotionally and reinforces our negative instinctual tendency toward cruelty.

Since our inherited tendencies toward kindness/cruelty form the terrestrial basis of good/evil in human nature, there is a direct connection between our basic instinctual need for affection/esteem/approval and the fruit of good/evil choices. This connection comes into play in the dramatic context of how people choose to treat each other in all types of relationships, and in terms of how we choose to treat our self. How we are treated strongly influences how we tend to treat others; and how we treat others affects how we treat our self. Are we kind or cruel, sincere or deceptive toward others and our self? Do we like and accept others for who they are or only those who agree with and support our personal agenda?

Our emotional need for affection/esteem/approval may be met both outwardly and inwardly. Outwardly, it may be met through relationships with important others in our life, through acceptance and approval in society, and via conformity to the beliefs, values and expectations of our culture. Inwardly, this need may be met by developing self-respect and healthy self-esteem, and through our personal relationship to God and the eternal values of love, truth and freedom for all. In early life we look outside our self to others for affection, esteem and approval and it's only as we grow to maturity and become our own person that we learn to find the fulfillment of this need in our self and in relation to God.

Our need for affection/esteem/approval from others is extreme in the early years of life when we are most dependent and vulnerable. The degree of our vulnerability and need in this area in later life depends on two interrelated factors. These are, 1) how our need for affection/esteem/approval has been met or not met up until now, and 2) the level of our corresponding emotional health, maturity or immaturity. The healthy meeting of our need for affection/esteem/approval tends to empower us, fostering our emotional growth, independence, maturity and self-confidence; the denial or abuse of this need tends to retard our emotional growth, making us needy and undermining our self-confidence in relation to both self and others.

The vital importance of our need for affection/esteem/approval cannot be overstated. This was demonstrated in an experiment done with two baby rhesus monkeys I read about years ago in an introductory psychology textbook in college. Two healthy baby monkeys were separated from their mothers and placed alone in cages. The physical needs of each were provided for identically; that is, they were given adequate food, shelter and a comfortable cage to live in. The purpose of this experiment was to determine if non-physical attention and support would affect the health and wellbeing of the monkeys. So one monkey was picked up, held, hugged, smiled at and spoken to affectionately at feeding time, and the other monkey was fed but treated with emotional indifference.

The results in this experiment were dramatic; the monkey that was given positive emotional support thrived and the monkey that was ignored emotionally wasted away and died within a couple months, in spite of having its physical security/survival/safety needs fully met. These results were not what the experimenters expected. They expected both monkeys to do well. The researchers were forced to conclude that, for some unknown reason, the emotional nurturing of positive affection/esteem/approval from its caretaker is a requirement for health, growth, wellbeing, and survival in these primates. This same principle extends as well to humans, who need emotional affirmation and wellbeing for peace of mind, positive self-regard and the healthy development of conscience.

As the above experiment with baby rhesus monkeys, and years of human psychotherapy, from Sigmund Freud to Abraham Maslow and beyond demonstrate, we are born emotionally helpless and dependent on others to meet our need for affection/esteem/approval in early life. Meaning comes with caring. Human development, from birth onward, is a continuing process of psychological growth, social learning, cultural conditioning, and, hopefully, some degree of spiritual awakening or growth in love.

Kindness affirms both giver and receiver and always says "Yes" to life. On the other hand, cruelty, fear and disdain negate both giver and receiver and say "No" to life, moving us toward separation, loneliness and the fourth Fruit of the Fall. The isolation and incompleteness of duality are essential qualities of our human ground's "fallen state." From this arise our separate-self sense and the four Fruits of the Fall, especially our existential aloneness/incompleteness apart from God. Duality and separation create the primal existential perspective of human ground's "fallen state." It is in this context that our hungry hole in the soul and deep need for affection/esteem/approval arise.

How we are treated teaches us how life is. To whatever degree we are given positive affection/esteem/approval in early life and beyond, we experience life as good and our self as cared for and valued by those around us. This precious gift nurtures the bright seed of kindness in our soul and forms the basis for our developing kindness toward others and healthy self-esteem. On the other hand, to whatever degree our need for positive affection/esteem/approval goes unmet or is abused, the results will be the opposite of this and our world will seem darkly different.

In addition to being an emotional need in the soul, our need for affection/esteem/approval is also a social need, since we obviously receive much of our affection/esteem/approval from others in the context of human relationships. In this regard, identifying with and successfully adapting to the basic requirements of our native culture and society (or whatever one we happen to be in) become essential prerequisites for meeting our need for affection/esteem/approval in the area of group memberships and personal relationships. The herd instinct of conformity to the ways of our group and peers tells us to follow the lead of others and the guidance of cultural conditioning so we can "fit in" to our group.

### III

As infants and toddlers, hopefully we are introduced to the preciousness of love by receiving loving affection and care from our mother or other primary caregiver(s). This nourishing touch of kindness shows us the goodness of life, bonds us to our mother and, by extension, to the whole human family, teaching us through intimate experience that life and people are good. This positive bonding may then be carried over and appropriately expressed in all our subsequent relationships.

At some point in early life, as our consciousness of self and other develops, we learn to feel and express the preciousness of love toward others. This important development is the beginning of our spiritual empowerment in human ground.

The growth of our inner spiritual empowerment gradually frees us from childish emotional limitations and attachments, bringing us into the fullness of healthy maturity. Our spiritual growth in human ground is a step-by-step, life-long process unfolding according to the secret workings of its own inner law. It is essentially our growth in love, the wellspring of our spiritual ground.

Before we can learn to express love to others in early life and beyond, we need to receive it from them, like a candle's wick receiving flame from the burning wick of another candle that touches it. Once our wick of love is lit and we keep it burning, then we can freely give its flame to others. Then we can share the love within us with whomever we wish.

Once we receive love and our heart responds with love, keeping the flame alive, then the wick of love in our soul may, by God's grace, come to receive flame directly from its inner Source and spiritual ground. Hence, our need for affection/esteem/approval, which is ultimately our need for love, begins as a need for emotional security and support, and ends in the fulfillment of love growing in our soul. It is initially the need to be valued by others and to value our self. Ultimately, it becomes our need for intimacy/belonging and love divine.

## IV

Throughout life, we all have a natural need for positive self-regard, to respect and love our self in a mature, healthy way. This is what's meant by "healthy self-esteem." Healthy self-esteem is based on living in harmony with authentic human and spiritual values (conscience) and is not the same thing as childish egotism and selfishness, or as having too high an opinion of oneself. Humility, as an attitude of honesty and gratitude toward reality, God and others, is a hallmark of healthy self-esteem. A core aspect of such humility is realizing we are not self-sustaining beings but dependent for existence on a life and consciousness inconceivably greater than our separate-self sense of ego-identity.

Healthy self-esteem helps us meet our need for affection/esteem/approval without being overly dependent on the opinions of others. To like or love oneself in this way, one needs to be a person who honestly feels worthy of one's own respect and love. That is, we have to live up to our own personal standards and values, which usually begin in human ground as the internalized standards and values of parents, peers, society, and cultural conditioning. We tend to rely on what we've internalized from outside until we mature to the point where we come to know our innate conscience and learn to think and decide things for our self.

To make the moral/ethical standards, beliefs, and values we've internalized from parents and culture truly our own, we have to think them through, weigh them and then decide for our self, in consultation with conscience, what we are to truly value and believe. Then, to respect our self genuinely, we need to live our life and treat others in harmony with our chosen beliefs and values. Our conscience is the best guide we can have in this. No one else can do it for us or give us the self-respect that comes from living true to our self. And no one else can take this away from us. We alone have the power to create or destroy our healthy self-esteem, each for one's self.

The ultimate fulfillment of our need for affection/esteem/approval comes through following our innate conscience and actively developing a living connection to spiritual ground. It's on the spiritual level that we are most fully and truly known (by the divine consciousness), and it's here that we may most truly and fully know our self. The divine presence knows us through and through and reveals us to our self in the secret "inner room" of our soul where we may humbly listen in deep prayer and meditation.[1]

Affection/esteem/approval is a many-faceted need. Its diverse dimensions in relation to self, others and God wend their winding ways throughout the course of human life, following the continual transforming dance of death/change. They are with us from the dependencies of infancy, childhood, and adolescence through the comparative independence and self-reliance of adulthood. Our need of affection/esteem/approval intertwines with the fruit of sex/desire in our searching quest for heart's treasure. In the course of this quest, we meet with the fruit of good/evil choices and their consequences time and again.

The ways of kindness and goodness bring us closer to our soul's goal where the quest for enduring affection/esteem/approval ends in love's fulfillment flowering whole in spiritual ground. Here we are never alone or incomplete. On the other hand, the ways of cruelty, ignorance and evil divide us from our inner goal, leading us darkly under the shadow of dreaded existential aloneness/incompleteness apart from God. Here we are never content but ever empty, restless, aching and apart from the love of our heart. How truly it's been said that the most honored and fortunate person is he or she who has true self-knowledge and with it good cause to value, love and respect one's true self.

## 7

## OUR BASIC NEEDS, PART THREE

### POWER/CONTROL, INTIMACY/BELONGING

I

The evolution of creation's life-force energy in humans moves up from the physical-instinctual and vital-sensate realms into the emotional and mental levels. These four levels of evolving life-force energy correlate to the development of our first four basic instinctual needs: security/survival/safety, sensation/pleasure, affection/esteem/approval and power/control. Each succeeding development of creation's life-force energy grows out of the energy on the levels that precede it. Hence, our basic need for power/control emerges from the energy of our need for affection/esteem/approval, which itself evolves out of our needs for security/survival/safety and sensation/pleasure. The conditions and energies of our basic instinctual needs all interact and react upon one another.

The ideal foundation for developing our need for power/control is meeting the basic instinctual needs that precede and underlie it. This gives one a calm state of inner peace, contentment, and wellbeing. Relative peace of mind and emotional wellbeing are required for optimal cognitive development. Peace of mind comes from having our legitimate needs met and living in harmony with our conscience. On this basis, we may enjoy clarity of thought and healthy expression of our need for power/control.

Human power/control depends on accurate knowledge of reality (truth), our practical skills, and abilities, and is essentially our need to be free. Power/control is our legitimate need for personal freedom and independence in human ground; that is, our need for freedom to choose our friends, direction in life and to be our own person by living true to our higher values. In the course of growing up, our need for power/control evolves through human ground into spiritual ground. That is, it evolves from our need to become a healthy, mature, autonomous adult in society into discovering and becoming our true self as a spiritual being in relation to God.

Healthy power/control in human ground concerns our free will and ability to discriminate and choose between good and evil. Without this ability, our free will is mostly an illusion. On the level of spiritual ground, power/control is our need to become united to God's divine will in relation to our self and created reality. Natural Law, which we may also call Cosmic Spiritual Law, expresses God's Will and is the ultimate power/control governing created reality. This Law is the practical means for fulfilling the divine plan to perfect God's creation by awakening all evolving consciousness into the inconceivable love, truth, and freedom of non-created Reality.

To give attention to something is to give it energy, life, and power. In this way, we each exercise our power/control by focusing our lens of consciousness to create our own subjective reality. The less mentally developed we are, the more we are liable to focus on what is of immediate emotional importance to us without weighing our priorities in terms of the future. Though living the now-moment is essential to spiritual awareness, fixation on immediate gratification at the expense of a larger perspective is generally a sign of emotional or mental immaturity. When such a one-sided bias appears, it indicates a deficiency in the freedom and efficiency of our personal power/control. That is, it indicates that we may be unaware of what we really want or need, and of what's most important in the long run, especially when emotional happiness programs, temptations, and good/evil choices are involved.

Our personal power/control is our ability to function and get along on all levels of life. The power/control we gain from language, conscience and our mental development allows us to become appreciative of time, true values, and what we may need or want in the future. This perspective is crucial for developing healthy power/control. It separates the short-term demanding consciousness of childhood and adolescence from the more mature, patient and balanced awareness of an adult. Sometimes it seems we must choose between enjoying life like a carefree child versus being responsible like a more grown-up and serious adult or parent figure. This may be the case for a time, while we're in the process of growing up emotionally and mentally, but it's ultimately not the case as we reach true integrated maturity in human and spiritual ground.

A healthy, empowered adult recovers and retains the child's ability to enjoy creative spontaneity and living in the present moment while integrating this into a perspective on moral/ethical values and long-term worthy goals. In other words, healthy mental development based on emotional maturity gives us the best of both worlds. It gives us the immediacy of living freely, consciously and presently in the subjective now, plus an objective time frame perspective on the overall big picture of our life. From such an integrated perspective, we may enjoy healthy power/control and freedom to exercise good judgment in our life choices.

## II

Certain attributes of power/control are instrumental in allowing us to meet our basic instinctual needs. For example, the various abilities, gifts, skills and talents we possess form an integral part of our personal power/control; and these assets may be used to help us understand and meet our physical, vital, emotional, mental, psychic, social and spiritual needs. Meeting our needs, accomplishing our goals, and fulfilling our life are primary reasons for us to develop the healthy strengths and aspects of personal power/control. Chief among these on the moral/ethical level are self-control, giving freedom to others by accepting them as they are and allowing them to make their own, hopefully informed, life choices. That is, we need to honor the personal integrity, freedom, and power/control of others.

As stated earlier, our basic need for power/control is essentially our need for freedom, independence, life orientation, and self-determination. It's our need to discriminate between the opposites (like good/evil), to know our self and make conscious choices based on what we really need and want (sex/desire). The better we know our self, our choices, and their probable consequences, the wider is the range of our personal freedom.

We tend to use whatever abilities, talents, and skills we develop in human ground to pursue sex/desire, cope with death/change, make good/evil choices and avoid or overcome our aloneness/incompleteness. What we want and where we focus our attention form the central point of power/control in each human soul. This point of power/control may be focused on good or evil choices, happiness programs, or spiritual goals. We may focus it sometimes on human ground and other times into spiritual ground.

In spiritual ground, our need for power/control is our need for inner alignment with our true self and the divine will of non-created Reality. This requires self-control and overcoming the conscious and unconscious counter tendencies of our immature false self. Mature, healthy power/control means having self-control, discrimination, and restraint in how we use our abilities, talents and skills to get what we want. It means having wisdom and using our power/control in ways that support the primal will to good (true conscience).

We become aligned with our true self by consenting to and cooperating with healthy death/change as manifested by Natural Law and the divine action in us and in our life. Our consenting and cooperating with the divine action is to be carried forward step by step until we finally surrender the self-centered will of our false separate-self over to the God-centered will of our true self. By surrendering to the ways of divine love, truth, and freedom, we ultimately come to participate in the universal power/control of the divine as co-creators with God.

Meeting our need for power/control in spiritual ground is the life-long project of our inner spiritual growth and transformation (death/change). During the course of this process, we gradually come to share more and more in the grace of divine consciousness and the ultimate power/control of God in service to the divine plan for both our self and all creation. Fulfillment of our need for power/control in spiritual ground gives us freedom to be our true self. Inner peace and goodwill toward others, humility, patience, kindness, and compassion: these are signs of power/control in our spiritual ground. Their fruits are the continuing growth, enrichment, and expansion of love, truth and freedom in our soul.

## III

Intimacy/belonging is the need we feel in relation to what's important and closest to us in heart and mind. This includes our self and God, as well as other persons and the culture with which we identify. Intimacy/belonging gives us a sense of rootedness and identity wherever we invest our caring in both human ground and spiritual ground. More than anything else, intimacy/belonging and the love it engenders are capable of filling in the hole in our soul. Meeting or not meeting our need for intimacy/belonging makes all the difference between loneliness and love in how we subjectively experience our life in human ground.

Intimacy/belonging is an outer need and an inner need of the soul, a social need and a spiritual need. We develop a sense of belonging to our society and culture by identifying with them, which involves internalizing their beliefs and values as our own. This helps give us a sense of group identity and place to belong, as well as providing us a worldview and orientation to life shared by others around us. Like speaking the same language, it helps us to communicate with one another, bonding us in a common sense of group membership.

On a more individual level, we pursue fulfillment of our need for intimacy/belonging through close personal relationships. Here this need becomes our quest for friendship and love on a personal level with certain special people in our life. In the best cases, such relationships evolve from human friendships into spiritual friendships centered in God and mutual love. Such deep intimacy may occur in any type of relationship people share.

In Thomas Keating's conceptual background for Centering Prayer, four deepening levels of relationship are identified. They are called 1) acquaintanceship, 2) friendliness, 3) friendship and 4) full intimacy or union of life. These levels of relationship carry a kind of vulnerability/trust, risk/reward dynamic. Each deepening level of relationship offers rewards of increasing intimacy but requires of us a deeper level of commitment and trust in the other person because, with increasing intimacy comes increasing self-disclosure and vulnerability.

The risk/reward dynamic works like this: the deeper and more honest the self-disclosure and intimacy, the more authentic and rewarding the relationship may become for us, as we are seen and valued for whom we truly are. However, such deep self-disclosure carries with it increased vulnerability and risk of possible rejection or betrayal. It hurts the most when we are rejected or betrayed by those who know us well and in whom we've placed our trust. On the other hand, it fulfills us the most when we are authentically accepted and loved for who we truly are as a human person and in relation to God. "In the best and truest of friendships, highest priority is given to one another's growth in relation to God."[1]

We come to deeper levels of rewarding intimacy/belonging by opening our self to equally deeper levels of vulnerability and trust. This applies to our relationships with other people, with our self and to our relationship with God. However, there are some important differences among these categories of relationship. In human relationships, there is always at least a remote chance of suffering rejection or betrayal because people have free will, may change their minds and we can never know absolutely what someone else, or we our self will decide to do under unexpected circumstances. We cannot predict with complete certainty how the four Fruits of the Fall will affect others or our self amid life's surprising uncertainties. This curious fact of human life's uncertainty is an important part of what makes it such an interesting and dramatic adventure.

On the other hand, in our relationship with God there's no possibility of us suffering real rejection or betrayal because divine love is not subject to human errors and flaws. God's love for us is unconditional, eternal, pure and free from contamination by the fears, weaknesses and neurotic needs of a false self. At times, due to ignorance and doubts, we may mistakenly think God has rejected or abandoned us, as when our wishes or expectations are not met, or if we have no felt experience of the divine presence for what seems a long time. This is simply our weakness and lack of trusting faith in God.

Deepening our relationship with God always involves going through an inner purification and healing process to remove obstacles of immaturity and selfishness in us blocking our way to growing intimacy, communion, and union with God. This process of inner transformation (death/change) can only happen on God's terms because only God sees the whole picture and knows what needs to be done to bring our transformation about. It's up to us to trust, accept, and cooperate with the divine wisdom and action working in us and in our life.

As Thomas Keating has said, our transformation is God's work. Our job is simply to be faithful to our regular daily Centering Prayer or other spiritual practice while humbly consenting to being transformed (cooperating), and patiently putting up with afflictive emotions and other potential symptoms of the inner purification process or "unloading of the unconscious." The hard part of the job, our renewal in spiritual ground, is all God's responsibility. Getting through this process, which does not happen overnight, calls for sustained faithfulness, consent, trust and cooperation with the divine action on our part. It requires willingness to be led "where we do not want to go," and to accept whatever "dark nights of the soul" are needed for our inner healing, renewal and rebirth in spiritual ground. Like many things that are worthwhile in human life, this is much easier said than done.

## IV

The greatest fulfillment of our needs for affection/esteem/approval and intimacy/belonging comes through our developing intimacy with God. As our relationship with God deepens, we develop a growing intimate, living contact with the divine presence. A variety of secret affirmations of wellbeing and inspirations of preciousness may flow through us in the context of our growing inner relationship with God. These gratuitous graces, when they come, give us all the emotional support we need as we gradually come to share in the rich love, truth and freedom of divine energy moving within us. Intimacy involves caring, trusting, closeness and naked self-disclosure, before God or another person. It's a return to simple innocence in caring attentiveness to feelings and what's present in the immediate now moment.

As human relationships deepen, individuals become, to some degree, identified with each other. This moves them toward a felt sense of intimacy with and belonging to each other, a sense of caring oneness. In a similar, profounder way, the deepening of our relationship with God brings us into a sense of sacred intimacy and belonging to God. God, who already knows all about us, reveals and exposes us to our self on ever deepening levels of intimacy/belonging. This tends to bring us to greater humility and gratitude for the loving care and gracious goodness of our true God who gives us all that we have and are.

Intimacy/belonging in human relationships may be experienced on all levels of our being: physical, vital, emotional, mental, psychic, social, and spiritual. Feelings of intimacy/belonging between people may be shared and mutual or solitary and one-sided. Intimacy and connection on one level in a human relationship does not necessarily guarantee intimacy and connection on other levels. For example, two people having physical sex obviously share physical and vital-energy intimacy, but this may or may not also involve mutual intimacy on deeper levels. Two individuals experience intimacy/belonging together only on those levels of energy exchange where they care, are actively engaged, open and relating to each other in the present moment. This is a key point related to the interactions and energy exchanges in all our relationships.

The deep attraction for personal intimacy with another person we care for is a hope, promise or call for return to our Lost Paradise. Intimacy/belonging involves our need to truly know and be known, our need for a sense of home where we belong, are welcome, content and loved. On the deepest level, this is the longing of our soul for intimacy/belonging in spiritual ground. It's the hunger of our restless heart for that elusive place of fulfillment, peace and sweet repose beyond the ups and downs of a changing, uncertain life. It's natural for people to seek this ideal through all types of intimate personal relationships. The pinnacle of life's inspiration and fulfillment shines for us in the rewarding meaning and rich preciousness we discover when our needs for intimacy/belonging are met in human ground and spiritual ground.

## V

The experience of falling in love gives us instant feelings of intimacy/belonging, deep relatedness, and sudden glimpses of that heavenly, intimate place where we experience ourselves in divine presence and the divine presence in us, though we may not recognize it as such. Spiritually, romantic falling in love concerns much more than the instincts of sex/desire, which tend to be its focus in the appetites and attractions of our basic human ground. Love comes from spiritual ground and expresses through human ground as a call to deepening intimacy/belonging, its touch a taste of our Lost Paradise. The heavenly glimpses of divine preciousness falling in love gives, however brief they may be, reveal the inner potential of our spiritual ground, which is always present within and around us. The spontaneous awakening of love in our heart brings us instantly to the acme of intimacy/belonging, integrating human ground and spiritual ground in the sublime fulfillment of our deepest ideals, desires, and needs. Such intimacy/belonging is a door to the divine.

Love fulfills our need for intimacy/belonging because love invests its object with preciousness while uniting lover and beloved on the levels where they care. Union in love is the heart's essence of intimacy/belonging where to know is to love and to love is to become. Our transformation and growth in human ground is a continual becoming process. Since "to love is to become," we naturally internalize and identify with whom or whatever we love. To be intimately one with anyone or anything in love is the ultimate belonging because all true love connects us to the same divine ground and unites us, whether we realize this or not.

True intimacy overcomes the isolation and loneliness of the fourth Fruit of the Fall. In love's awakening light, we lose our separate-self to find our new and true self, created in the divine image of oneness alive. This is the highest ideal and potential of our growing in love through intimacy/belonging. Its unspoken promise is an intimation of Paradise that calls and attracts us through all the labyrinths of sex/desire in human ground and beyond.

To remain in the magical transformation and intimacy/belonging of love's precious gift, we need to live in harmony with it. We need to allow love to shape us into its perspective on life and reality. We are unable to sustain love in our consciousness and relationships because we try to possess it with our ego or false self. We try to manipulate love to our agenda rather than allowing our self to be conformed to the way and will of love. This is the unknowing folly of our false self in human ground. Therefore, losing the wonderful magic, we wonder where has love gone? What did I do wrong?

How quickly and easily we lose the grace of love's presence in our soul, its beautiful feeling alive in our body! This is due to spiritual immaturity, blindness and unwillingness to learn from love. Unaware of our error regarding love, we may succumb to doubting its enduring goodness, blaming another or love itself for our failure to live and grow in love. So how may love grow in the temporary time of our human ground and relationships? The answer to this question depends on the spirits in which we act and react going forward where love attracts love and "like attracts like."

Feelings come and go as moods change and desires grow or fade away. Seeking to possess the eternal in the transitory does not work, as love slips from our grasp like grains of sand in the desert of time. At best, we catch passing glimpses of our Lost Paradise in the fleeting glow of beauty's beaming shadow. Yet, if we humble our self to love and identify with the love we find in human ground, living true to its inspiration, we may then come to belong to love and this will free us. Love has been well-designated "its own reward." "Learn from me," says Christ, Lord of Love, "for I am gentle and humble of heart" (Matthew 11:29).

Work has been called "love made visible."[2] Sustaining love in human relationships requires a special kind of work that outgrows the false self's childish "me first" attitudes. In committed human relationships, deeply involved intimacy combined with caring faithfulness open the door to enduring love in human ground. Such relationships are not easy and may be rare in our lives. They require mutual commitment, forgiveness, and mutual effort. Yet the promise of their potential speaks to us in the mirror of beauty's caring smile whenever we behold it or share for a moment in the presence of love.

Just a touch, a taste of love's sacredness redeems, if only briefly, the hollow emptiness and loneliness of life in fallen human ground. Love's effortless awakening in the soul lifts us instantly, magically into the precious fullness of timeless revelation, filling us with wordless wonder and rewarding meaning in spiritual ground, rich and intimate beyond all other treasures we may know in this passing world. It lifts us to the freedom place of forever, of ultimate intimacy/belonging in awakening presence of the divine, whether we know it or not. Love is the sum of all beauty, the heart of all goodness.

True intimacy reveals beauty, and beauty intimacy. No wonder we are so attracted, moved and captured by beauty before us, in whatever form: physical, vital, emotional, moral, mental, psychic, social or spiritual. Beauty beheld is a mirror of spiritual ground whispering of our Lost Paradise, heart's treasure to find. Beauty in all its variety and wonder throughout creation is the living signature of God's divine intimacy/belonging, touching our soul and calling us home. Love, sum of all beauty, is the deepest intimacy and love unites, making us one and whole in the magic of its preciousness. In love's oneness, we belong and are intimate to the point of actual co-participation and shared identity. Hence, our life in divine love is the ultimate fulfillment of our need for intimacy/belonging.

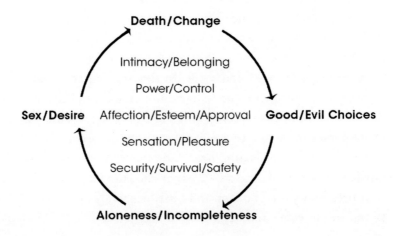

8

# FALSE SELF AND HAPPINESS PROGRAMS, PART ONE

I

Not knowing the truth of our soul and spiritual ground, we mistakenly relate to Fruits of the Fall and our basic instinctual needs from the blind, confused perspective of fallen human ground. That is, we relate to the existential parameters of our life and to the needs and wants of our desire nature from various viewpoints of our false self. We experience our self as alone, needy and incomplete, cut-off from others, God, and the world around us. This is an experience we all share as humans. It's the archetypal experience of Adam and Eve after the fall from Paradise into human ground and separate-self consciousness.

The spiritually impoverished, dualistic perspective of this basic human-ground experience often leads us on a forced march down a lost trail of disappointments and tears. We try to find happiness in a self-centered desert of fleeting mirages, not knowing our real self or what we truly need and want. In this state of spiritual ignorance, poverty and confusion, the hungry hole in our soul craves and clamors for nourishment. Its screaming need beckons us endlessly onward in desperate quest for that elusive something our heart tells us will bring us fulfillment, lasting peace and plenty in the promised land of our Paradise Found: and so we experience the human predicament of pleasures and pains, hunger and hurt, desperation and need, longing for meaning, value and belonging in life.

We are all born hungry, with a deep yearning to find some kind of satisfaction and fulfillment. This yearning comes from our instinctual needs, from the hole in our soul and from the haunting memory of our Lost Paradise. We are born hungry, in need of kindness, love, care, and comfort. We are born already addicted to our preprogrammed needs, helplessly afflicted and utterly subject to the four Fruits of the Fall. We have no choice in this. It's our given human circumstance, the fate on our plate.

To grow, survive and thrive alive, our needs must be met, at least to some minimal degree, within the tightly closed box of the parameters of our existence. To begin with, we know neither the full extent of our needs nor the Fruits of the Fall. We know only our hunger, our various experiences and their seemingly random vicissitudes. Life is confusing here, in the land of good/evil choices where we understand neither ourselves nor our true condition as vulnerable humans. Here, we are in great need of some real education, to draw forth from within us the wealth and wisdom hidden in our soul.

Understanding the Fruits of the Fall and our basic instinctual needs may help us to know better our choices and where our vulnerability lies. It's as if our soul is unconsciously caught in a web of twisted knots woven from the living rope of our life-force energy and basic instinctual needs. These knots in our soul have been tied by negative early-life experiences of our basic needs, by the Fruits of the Fall, and by our reactions to traumatic events and the inevitable predicaments we face in human ground. To grasp our situation better, we need to know our weaknesses and their origins. To untie the web of twisted psychic knots that bind us, we need divine help, we need to trust that help and we need some understanding of how these knots were tied to begin with. The knots that bind and blind us are the basis of our false self, which is essentially a childish complex of unconscious compulsions, weaknesses and addictions (happiness programs) related to our basic instinctual needs.

The living rope containing human nature's basic instinctual needs is the divine life force of evolutionary energy within us (also known as the Serpent of Paradise or kundalini energy). This living rope is the central axis of our soul's energy-field and its presence and movements in us are mostly unconscious. What we generally experience consciously are the positive or negative effects created by the ongoing movements and tensions in our soul's energy-field. When the knots in our soul's axial rope are being untied, we experience a release or unloading of our unconscious psychic contents and the freeing effects of spiritual growth in us.

During the course of our inner purification, healing, and growth process, the blocks in our soul's energy-field are gradually freed, releasing the distortions and compulsions created by our childish happiness programs. As this transformation takes place, the energy centers of our basic instinctual needs unload their toxic contents and then open wide so life-force energy may flow freely through them. The vibrant rope of our life-force energy then blossoms into an invisible body of transformations and consciousness awakening, extending from the base of our spine to the top of our head and beyond. Our soul's rope of life-force energy and its progressive, healthy unfolding are central manifestations of our spiritual growth in human ground. The elan vital of this living rope is an essential aspect of our soul's deep mystery and functioning.

Out of this life-force rope, in conjunction with early life experiences and the Fruits of the Fall, the knots of destiny were tied, constricting our vital energy, and the web was woven to bind our soul in the primal bondage of human ground. This inevitable outcome of human limitation and suffering is our participation in the biblical Adam and Eve drama. It is also our potential participation in the paschal mystery of false-self death, redemption, and inner resurrection of our true self, symbolized by the passage of Jesus Christ from human into divine life.

Knots in our living rope of life-force energy have also come from our reactions to certain traumatic, painful early life events related to physical birth and our survival instinct. We were assailed by these traumatic experiences when we had no way to defend or protect ourselves from their overwhelming intensity and harshness. Experiences of utter helplessness, frustration, fear, rage, and uncertainty have marked us from our beginnings in human ground. The imprints of these powerful events create lasting impressions and compelling influences in each soul, brain, and nervous system born into human life.

## II

Our early sense of self develops around our instinctual needs and the drive to get them met. This early sense of self is totally self-centered and develops into our separate-self sense of ego-identity (false self) as we grow up. Our false self tends to be dominated by instinctual needs, happiness programs and by various positive and negative emotions that are activated when our deep-seated needs and desires are either frustrated or gratified.

These powerful emotions are also activated when we imagine that our needs are being frustrated or gratified. When needs are gratified, we experience pleasure and are programmed to want more when the need naturally arises. When needs are frustrated or abused, we experience pain and, to compensate, are programmed to want revenge and/or to demand exaggerated amounts of gratification beyond what our legitimate needs naturally require. In this way, a neurosis of psychic knots develops in our soul's energy-field, blocking our human and spiritual growth.

It works like this: when real or imagined frustration or abuse of basic instinctual needs is experienced in early life, the unbearable pain of these experiences is repressed into the unconscious. That is, whenever our needs were neglected, abused, or experienced as unmet, we were traumatized. Too painful and overwhelming to deal with, we repressed these experiences into unconsciousness to get away from them. The repressed experiences and our reactions were then coagulated into psychic knots of compacted energy buried and held in our physical body, nervous system and soul. These psychic knots of repressed feelings, experiences, and desires power the emotional happiness programs that drive our false self.

Since there is no passage of time in the unconscious, the pain of our repressed experiences of deprivation/abuse, and our primitive emotional reactions to them, remain exactly the same as when originally repressed, affecting us unconsciously as we grow up and move through life. This traps and retards our personal and emotional development, creating a continuing state of psychological bondage and subjecting us to domination by various afflictive emotions that go off when our happiness programs are frustrated or gratified.

Our false-self happiness programs attempt to resolve the knots in our energy-field by trying to fully and finally satisfy our unmet needs and wants, which have become distorted and exaggerated into unrealistic demands and fantastic expectations. These drives to compensate are powered by the strong emotions of pain and pleasure stored in our instinctual energy centers and physical body. Unchecked, our unconscious programs for happiness will dominate us for the rest of our lives, unless some deep healing takes place. This situation, to which we are all heirs via terrestrial evolution and the Fruits of the Fall, sets the stage for serious obstacles to our human and spiritual growth.

## III

Once established, self-centered emotional programs for happiness in our unconscious become top priorities for us. These happiness programs carry the full authority and intensity of our basic instinctual needs and tend to oppose higher human and spiritual values by ignoring true conscience and the legitimate rights and needs of others. They reinforce our egoistic selfishness and function as idolatrous substitutes for God. In other words, God takes a back seat to the unconscious happiness programs dominating our desire nature. We may or may not be conscious of this or of the fact that pursuing self-centered happiness programs as top priorities inevitably leads to moral/ethical compromises regarding how we treat others, our self and God.

Whenever we act out of neurotic happiness programs, or the afflictive emotions that arise when they're frustrated or gratified, rather than loosening the knots in our energy centers we are actually tightening them and strengthening their hold on us. This is fundamental to how the insidious, self-defeating process of bondage to evil functions in the soul. When we seek freedom and consciously decide to pursue the spiritual path, our self-centered emotional programs for happiness become primary obstacles to our inner growth.

They are like false goals or gods we worship (place preciousness into) that compete with the higher human and divine values of our conscience and spiritual ground. These childish programs for happiness are false because, as Thomas Keating says, "they can't possibly work." They are actually lies and programs for human slavery and misery. The unique complex of emotional happiness programs in each person forms the working core of her or his "false-self system." This false self is who we think we are but not who we really are. It's a "homemade self," as Keating says, and not the true self of our spiritual ground and life in God. The false self's innermost core is the primal illusion and obstacle of our absolute separate-self sense.

Our false self fails to perceive our connection to spiritual ground and our inner solidarity with others. It is not necessarily a bad or evil self, though it often inclines toward evil, obviously has serious limitations, and is a source of much misery. Generally, the false self is a combination of both good and evil qualities and tendencies, a mixture of plus and minus points. The false self is what makes us vulnerable to temptations to evil but also gives us the option of choosing the good. It is our human personality and separate-self sense minus any living conscious connection to our spiritual dimension and true self.

Our false self is an incomplete self, a needy self, an unevolved self, and a temporary self. It's a spiritually ignorant self, trapped under the hypnotic spell and illusion of absolute ego-identity. This illusion of ego-identity is generally accepted as a given fact of human life and supported by cultural conditioning as "consensus reality" in human society and relationships. Belief in this unfounded root-assumption is the basis of the false self's identity in society and its bondage to itself. Ultimately, our changing and impermanent false self, though possessing relative reality as a factual illusion, is something that we have: but it's not who or what we truly are as spiritual beings. Our basic error consists in over-identification with it as our self.

Our false self develops out of our learned sense of identity in human ground. Associated from early on with our separate-self survival instinct, we tend to trust and rely on our false self like a dear friend. It is indeed something that we have (like a friend or enemy), but it's also something that has us caught relatively helpless in its grasp. It has us like this because we unconsciously come to identify it with whom or what we truly and ultimately are. This miss-identification with our false self is the basic tragic flaw of human self-ignorance.

Each person's false-self system consists of the specific self-centered motivations and happiness programs he or she has developed from early life. These secret unconscious agendas constitute the false self's automatic-habit programming patterns and have been developed around each person's wounded, distorted and exaggerated needs for security/survival/safety, sensation/pleasure, affection/esteem/approval, power/control and intimacy/belonging. From this, we may picture the false self as our central, separate self-identity surrounded by its satellites, which are its governing emotional programs for survival and happiness.

Imagery plays a powerful role in human psychology. Our false self's happiness programs are based on the subjective dream-logic of unconscious symbolism where one person or thing (e.g., food) is unconsciously equated with another (e.g., love). New desires, roles, and goals are incorporated into our false self and its happiness programs as we grow up and adapt to new circumstances. As our conditions change, unconscious symbol substitutions are typically made to accommodate them; that is, new players and objects in our personal drama tend to replace former ones that become inappropriate, unavailable, or unworkable in our new circumstances.

As this occurs, the underlying unconscious agendas and games of the false self remain the same, in spite of things, including ourselves, appearing to be different on the surface. On the subjective level of dream-logic symbolism, all people, places, and things are potentially interchangeable and may be used for acting-out the false self's pre-existing patterns. For example, as Freud discovered, we learn from our parents on many levels and a child's father or mother is typically identified unconsciously with her or his adult husband or wife, as protector, nurse, source of affection/love, caretaker, authority figure, fantasy lover, and so forth.

We tend to treat others as we were treated growing up, and we tend to want from others what we wanted (but may not have gotten) from our parents and other significant people earlier in life. Our parents were our first teachers and role models, and we all have strong inclinations to imitate them in later life, often believing and appearing to be quite different from our parents. This is one of those ironic jokes of the unconscious we play on ourselves when we deny and repress unresolved issues related to early life and our parents. Such jokes, which are generally quite sad, are created by our false self in its attempts to compensate for earlier-life shortcomings.

The phenomenon of unconscious symbol substitution is liable to happen in any type of situation or relationship. Whenever it does happen, past feelings and relationships are unconsciously projected and acted-out upon present tense players in our real life dramas, adding further dimensions and complexities to our false self's activities and happiness programs. New developments in roles and relationships experienced as we grow up and live our lives are progressively layered onto preexisting patterns in the knots and energy centers of our instinctual needs. Like a chameleon that changes its colors to suit changing circumstances, the false self is capable of adapting to any and all situations, roles, and relationships.[1] What is most empowering to the false self and its unhealthy happiness programs is our conscious ignorance and denial of their functioning within us.

The perceived reality of the false self is reinforced by the perceived reality of our unconscious symbolic associations, happiness programs, and life dramas. The games played by the false self are the pursuit of its desires. Since the drama of its games seems so real, then it stands to reason that the player of those games, i.e., our false self, must also be real. This "proof" of its reality overlooks the fact that each game played by the false self is a made up thing, a factual illusion based on assumptions of duality, fantasy, and drama. Absolute duality perceived in desire's longing, i.e., the separation between "me" and what I want, is a time-dependent foundation of our false self. In contrast to this, absolute unity experienced in love's fulfillment is a timeless presence revealing our true self.

Drama is created by attachment to outcomes; as caring creates meaning in human life, so does attachment to results create drama. Our dramas and what we care about may be of either the false self or the true self. This depends on good/evil choices, our motivations, goals and what we've learned. Wanting something, having a personal agenda, creates drama in our life. Will we get it or not? From this we may appreciate the central role of sex/desire in human life. The false self's inner patterns tend to remain the same until they are gradually transformed, outgrown, and eliminated by the healing process of divine grace working in our soul, which, of course, requires our willing consent and cooperation.

## IV

As we've seen in previous chapters, our basic needs are all legitimate, good, and necessary within their natural spheres of expression. It's only when they become distorted and exaggerated into unrealistic emotional happiness programs (psychic knots), complete with afflictive emotions that go off when they're frustrated, that they become a problem. Since we need security/survival/safety on all levels, e.g., physical, vital, emotional, etc., we are liable to develop corresponding happiness programs on all these levels and in conjunction with other basic instinctual needs. We shall see some examples of these in following sections of this book.

Our physical security/survival/safety needs for food, shelter, clothing, exercise, and rest are quite obvious. When this need is distorted and exaggerated into emotional happiness programs on the physical level, there is a compelling drive to acquire more and more personal and cultural symbols of physical security/survival/safety. We may be driven to pursue more and more material wealth, luxury, food, clothes, cars, houses, toys, insurance policies, and medical assurances regarding our health and longevity. Unconsciously, and to some degree consciously, acquiring more and more of these things is identified with happiness, wellbeing and feeling secure. Unfortunately, acquiring more and more does not change the childish program for happiness in the unconscious. Thus, no matter how much we may amass, it'll never be enough. Like any addict, we keep on craving more and more.

If we don't get what we want to gratify our security/survival/safety program, then we suffer various afflictive emotions, such as the fear, panic, rage, hunger, or insecurity that engendered the compulsion in the first place. To compensate for this, we may be unconsciously driven to act-out our inner feelings of insecurity and lack by engaging in such behaviors as hoarding things, becoming miserly or pursuing the futility of compulsive eating to fill up the hole in our soul. We may become kleptomaniacs, compulsively stealing things we don't really need or we may become anxious hypochondriacs, tormenting ourselves with frightful imaginings regarding our personal health and safety. These are all signs of unmet security/survival/safety needs.

On the other hand, if we do get what we want (e.g., more money, food, a new possession), our feeling of gratification will be relatively short lived because the unconscious happiness program motivating us is insatiable. As the novelty of our latest acquisition wears off, we'll find our self again wanting something else that's newer or better. As various temporary false-self dramas and delights may momentarily hide the hole in our soul, only real love can truly fill it in.

Security/survival/safety happiness programs involving material greed may lead us into patterns of compulsive consumption, financial irresponsibility, dishonesty, and increasing anxiety/insecurity. For example, we often hear reports in the news of prominent individuals in business, government and elsewhere who already have more wealth than they need getting caught committing crimes of deception and greed to acquire still more. Such unfortunate people are very likely compelled by pathological security/survival/safety happiness programs to behave in this way. They may also enjoy the dramatic excitement and thrills of taking risks (sensation/pleasure) or derive a sense of unhealthy power/control from grabbing what they want in defiance of others, the law and getting away with it. Those getting away with it, of course, would be the ones we don't hear about in the news. From this, we can see that the fruit of good/evil choices often enters into dramas of security/survival/safety happiness programs, along with other issues like financial sanity and security.

The insufficiency of all false-self happiness programs comes from their inability to restore our lost connection to spiritual ground, which alone can fulfill us; and it comes from our instinctual separate-self fear of physical death. The lurking fruit of inevitable death/change forms a major, inescapable source of unconscious, if not conscious anxiety related to our basic need for security/survival/safety. We each need to come to terms with the fact that we are vulnerable human beings who are subject to death/change and the other Fruits of the Fall. We ignore this fact at our own peril, perpetuating our ignorance of real life.

Until we make peace with the fact of our inevitable physical death, we're not free to truly live or find peace of mind. We'll probably continue to have security/survival/safety issues until our innate fear of death is resolved. Making peace with death is really not a physical problem at all but a spiritual one with a spiritual solution. As we've seen, the ultimate answer to our security/survival/safety needs, beyond physical life and death, rests in the truth of our soul, in our relationship to God and our continuing life in spiritual ground.

V

Our need for sensation/pleasure helps us awaken to self-consciousness, arousing our hunger and thirst for life. As our need for stimulation, sensation/pleasure is an area where we may distort what is good and natural to enjoy into unrealistic emotional programs for happiness. Tendencies toward overindulgence and addiction to various forms of sensation/pleasure are the basic pitfalls of its happiness programs. When we fail to learn the delicate art of conscious pleasure, we fall into errors of false-self greed, lust, and overindulgence, or into puritanical self-suppression and rejection of life's legitimate pleasures.

Whenever we pursue an emotional happiness program, we expect and demand of it more than it can possibly give us, no matter how much we indulge, distort, enjoy, or abuse it. The fruit of sex/desire is directly related to sensation/pleasure and plays a central role in all our appetites and pursuits to meet this need. Though many of the pleasures we desire are discovered through experience, all our basic instinctual needs are preprogrammed desires we are born with and all may be sources of sensation/pleasure for us. Our various pursuits of sensation/pleasure may be freeing or addicting, depending on how we go about indulging them.

Experiences of sensation/pleasure in which more than one basic instinctual need is met leave strong and lasting imprints in our soul, especially in early life. For example, as nursing infants, we enjoyed wonderful experiences of being fed and loved by our mother as our needs for physical security/survival/safety, vital sensation/pleasure, emotional affection/esteem/approval and spiritual intimacy/belonging were all met at the same time. That was like a return to our Lost Paradise where we are safe, warm, loved and all our needs are taken care of. The imprinted memory of such an experience leaves a deep, lasting impression in the soul, though it typically remains buried in the unconscious. It also forms an unconscious association linking receiving nourishing food to receiving emotional/spiritual nourishment (affection, esteem, and love). This unconscious food-love identification is known to play a key role in certain eating disorders and compulsions (unconscious happiness programs) that are psychological in origin.[2]

## VI

Happiness programs stored in the unconscious from early life tend to be acted out in external life on the symbolic stage of hidden associations and correspondences that equate one thing (e.g., food) with another (e.g., love). The secret code for these unconscious associations and correspondences is the psyche's subjective dream-logic symbolism based on instinctual memory, intuition, early life impressions, and other past experiences. Consciously, we have little clue as to what we're actually doing or why we're doing it. We just know, for example, that we want to eat that food, to enjoy more and more of it right now, chasing pleasure's peak to fill our self. We want to merge and become one with it in an ecstatic experience of sensation/pleasure stimulating our senses and touching our soul.

We may try to lose our self in the lust of compulsive eating, drinking, sex, drugs, gambling or whatever. Craving more, more and more, we overindulge because we just can't quite seem to ever get enough to fully fill our need, our hole in the soul. Such passionate, excessive behavior with food, or anything else, is more an unconscious desperate search for self-transcendence and oneness than it is a realistic attempt to meet any legitimate physical or psychological needs. On the surface, we may label such behavior as simple escapism, seeking "cheap thrills" and/or self-medication to get away from our present painful or boring reality by changing how we feel in the immediate moment; and these judgments may be quite accurate on their own levels.

On a deeper level, however, such blind, pitiful, and seemingly pathetic attempts to find self-transcendence in the fleeting moment by way of sensory overindulgence and, in some cases, oblivion are actually unconscious efforts to fulfill a profound spiritual need for mystical union with our spiritual ground.[3] This is also, on a deep unconscious human-ground level, a symbolic attempt to return to our Lost Paradise and the ecstatic intimacy of fusion with our mother's nourishing and loving breast and body. No wonder these addictions (e.g., food, alcohol, sex, drugs, etc.) are so compelling and difficult to overcome; they are much more than simply a "chemical dependency." They are also unconscious emotional, psychological, and spiritual addictions.

When our need for sensation/pleasure is distorted and exaggerated into an emotional program for happiness, this may manifest through various forms of expression, ranging from the sensual into the emotional, dramatic, and psychological. Intensity of experience (created by contrasts) will be pursued in terms of increasing both the quantity and the quality of whatever we indulge in to give us sensation/pleasure. Our unconscious search for transcendence demands this because no matter how far we go, we're never quite there yet, and we feel compelled to go further, to keep seeking the more and the better. This inevitably leads into overindulgence, abuse, loss of self-control and the slavery of addiction. Our life may be taken over by compulsive pursuits of sensation/pleasure focused on excesses in sex, drugs, food, alcohol, entertainment, physical danger, competitive sports, relationship dramas, suspense, and so forth. We may also be seduced into the dark, dangerous delights of ego-inflation, self-delusion, and sadomasochistic perversion.

The urgency and priority given to sensation/pleasure happiness programs cause us to lose balance in our overall perspective on life.

Obsession with personal addictions, no matter what they may be, tends to damage our life, health, and relationships. We mistakenly believe we must have whatever it is we're addicted to, if we're to be content or happy. Hence, we become psychological slaves to personal addictions, if not physical slaves. This degrading condition weakens us, destroys peace of mind, and strips us of our inherent dignity, integrity, and freedom as human beings. It divides us from our own true self, turning us into weak, groveling human beings, dependent on externals and desperate for a "quick fix."

All our happiness programs are the misguided agendas of the false self. In pursuing them, we become worshippers of lesser gods whose unrelenting commandments are our childish emotional happiness programs. The misguided false self and its happiness programs that can't possibly work fit the basic criteria of evil, as defined in this book. That is, they are lies because they cannot give us true happiness but lead into errors resulting ultimately in frustration, disappointment, addiction and suffering. These programs addict and enslave, depriving us of authentic love, truth and freedom, compelling us to act them out and subjecting us to various afflictive emotions that come to dominate us, destroying our peace and skewing our view of reality. Throughout this enslaving process, false-self happiness programs lead us into various physical and psychological habit patterns that can ruin our life and relationships. The end results of such frustration, humiliation and defeat may either be self-hatred, hatred and blame projected onto others or, after "hitting bottom," our conversion to a new way of life.

What's truly good for us contributes to our health and wellbeing. What is not harms and destroys them. In the realm of life's pleasures, it's not so much what we use or enjoy as the ways in which we use and enjoy that make the difference between healthy and unhealthy sensation/pleasure. What some Buddhists call "wisdom and skillful means" comprise what we need for optimum, healthy sensation/pleasure. The art of healthy pleasure requires us to simply slow down, be present and appreciate what we're experiencing.

# 9

# FALSE SELF AND HAPPINESS PROGRAMS, PART TWO

I

In early life and throughout childhood, meeting our need for affection/esteem/approval is crucial for our emotional security/survival/safety and wellbeing. This need serves to support and reassure us while we're growing up and learning to face life's issues. Seeing that others accept and value us helps us to accept and value our self. Our emotional need for affection/esteem/approval helps prepare us for the realization of our deeper spiritual need for intimacy/belonging.

In the face of our innate existential aloneness/incompleteness, we may naively look to affection/esteem/approval as an answer to this core human dilemma. When we do, we may exaggerate and distort this basic instinctual need into unrealistic emotional programs for happiness. We may consciously or subconsciously believe something like: If only I were famous, powerful, better looking, richer, smarter, or more talented; then people would love me, and I'd be happy. Or if only I had that perfect, loving intimate relationship, if people or at least someone needed me, or if I were number one, then I'd be loved and admired, people would like me and my life would be all I want it to be.

We may imagine various scenarios in which receiving affection/esteem/approval from others would make us happy and keep us safe from fears of rejection, incompleteness, and loneliness, but these are only vain imaginings, hypothetical ego-fantasies. What we ultimately need is not going to come to us from outside, from external people, places, or things. It has to come up from deep within us, from our true self and connection to spiritual ground.

When our need for affection/esteem/approval is abused or not adequately met, inner psychological damage and emotional retardation result. This may range from slight to severe wounding, and the resulting unconscious emotional happiness programs for compensation may be anywhere from moderate to extreme, depending on circumstances.

There are innumerable specific ways individuals may be wounded in their need for affection/esteem/approval, and equally as many variations of emotional happiness programs that may be created to compensate for this wounding. To get an overall idea of these, three general ways this need may be wounded are by neglect, rejection, and abuse. Responses to this emotional wounding may be either positive or negative. Positive responses are those where the individual creates an emotional happiness program to compensate by pursuing an inordinate amount of affection/esteem/approval. Negative responses are those where the individual rejects this need and acts-out against it. Let's look at some examples:

Individuals whose need for affection/esteem/approval was experienced as unmet in early life due to being left alone and neglected often do not like to be alone for any length of time, finding solitude boring, uncomfortable, depressing, or even threatening. In some cases, being alone may remind individuals of when their need for affection/esteem/approval was not met earlier in life. Children and adults craving attention to compensate for wounded emotional neediness and neglect will sometimes do almost anything to get it, preferring even negative attention (e.g., disapproval) to none at all.

When the need for affection/esteem/approval is wounded by real or imagined neglect, the person (particularly a child) becomes emotionally needy and may seek positive compensation by trying to get inordinate amounts of attention, recognition, and approval from peers or authority figures. Such unfortunate individuals are often haunted by low self-esteem and guilt, doubting their own worth and worthiness. To compensate, they may need continual reassurances, affirmations and reminders from others that they are liked, valued, loved, appreciated, needed, or cared for. To gain this compensation, such persons may go to great lengths, becoming "people pleasers" or over-achievers in various areas of human life and relationship.

As inner doubts continue to haunt them, low self-esteem individuals may feel compelled to keep "proving themselves," to others and to themselves, doing whatever they feel is necessary to accomplish this. They may become competitive or compliant, trying to impress or please by their performances or accomplishments. Unfortunately, whatever they do or achieve is never enough, so long as their wounded affection/esteem/approval happiness program remains active in the unconscious, repeating unrealistic demands to "prove oneself" and continuing to cry out for satisfaction. Neurotic perfectionism and obsession with what others think of us are examples of such negative, self-defeating happiness programs.

Individuals wounded by rejection in their need for affirmation and acceptance tend to seek positive compensation not only via continual reassurances from others (like those wounded by neglect), but also by needing to be wanted and needed as well. Being wanted and needed by others or another gives a feeling of power/control and serves as protection against the dreaded outcome of being rejected and left alone. Unconscious emotional happiness programs aimed at compensating for fears of rejection and abandonment can also make a person ripe for involvement in unhealthy codependent relationships where individuals reinforce each other's emotional neediness, insecurity, and programs for compensation.

One common example of seeking affection/esteem/approval via being wanted and needed is the "people pleaser." A people-pleasing person tends to focus on meeting the needs and wants of others while giving lower priority to one's own (other than the desire for exaggerated affection/esteem/approval). This is done as a kind of trade-off, to gain desperately needed positive attention, acceptance, and affection/esteem/approval. Focusing on the needs and desires of others may be seen as self-sacrificing virtue, a sign of unselfish maturity and independence rather than neediness, immaturity and dependency.

People who are too desperately eager to please others typically end up failing to please themselves as personal martyrdom for the sake of others' needs and wishes can easily become masochistic. Because their compulsive craving for attention and affection is so desperate, individuals who play a needy people-pleasing game are easily manipulated, dominated, used and taken advantage of by unscrupulous "friends" or lovers who exploit their emotional neediness and unconscious programming. At some point, the used or dominated people-pleasing person will come to resent both her/himself and the person who is taking advantage of their willingness and need to please. The results of such exploitation are always degrading and harmful for both parties involved in the process, which, if it continues, may degenerate into a depressing codependent, dysfunctional relationship.

At the same time, the emotionally needy people-pleasing person often manipulates her or his friends and partners by creating various kinds of unhealthy dependency in them, in order to feel needed, indispensable, and safe from rejection. Creating dependency and need in another person (who may have a complementary happiness program) serves as a kind of emotional insurance policy for individuals who are inwardly needy, insecure and in dreaded fear of rejection. Sometimes, fearing rejection brings up the memory and pain of past rejections.

Happiness programs grounded in fears of rejection, betrayal and abandonment typically make their subjects prone to domination by such afflictive emotions as possessiveness, jealousy, grief, insecurity, anger, suspicion, fear and doubt. These afflictive emotions, and others, are negative ways of compensating for wounded affection/esteem/approval needs that tend to make matters worse in human relationships by undermining mutual trust and introducing unnecessary conflicts. Acting out of these irrational afflictive emotions often ironically serves to sabotage a relationship and to bring about the very negative results the unwitting subject wishes to avoid. The interpersonal problem here seems to be based on lack of trust and false negative assumptions regarding the character and intentions of the other person.

Another negative response to fears of rejection, betrayal, and abandonment involves going on the offensive by playing the role of the person who does the rejecting, betraying or abandoning rather than allowing it to be done to oneself. This sad scenario, of course, assumes that the other person is going to reject, betray or abandon one if given the opportunity, the basic idea being that of a preemptive strike, i.e., "do it to them before they do it to you." Inability to trust and be vulnerable to another for fear of being hurt again is often the understandable inner weakness underlying this negative human relationship pattern.

Individuals whose need for affection/esteem/approval has been abused in early life are liable to seek negative compensation or revenge for this terrible experience in three basic ways: 1) by consciously or unconsciously seeking power/control over others (in order to control outcomes and feel safe). 2) They may seek compensation by becoming abusive to others in close relationships (unconsciously acting-out and taking revenge for their earlier wounding) or, 3) by entering into relationships where they become victims of abuse (symbolically re-creating the scenario in which they were originally wounded). In these examples, we can see how emotional abuse in early life (which may include physical, sexual, mental, psychic, or social abuse) can become a basis for sadomasochistic relationship patterns in later life. Unable to trust others, such unfortunate individuals only feel safe when they're in predictable situations or codependent relationships. On a still deeper level, beneath their unconscious neediness, vulnerability, insecurity and fear, individuals suffering from abused affection/esteem/approval needs desperately long for peace, acceptance and love. Not knowing this and being unable to reach out for it create great and continuing suffering in the soul.

## II

All emotional wounding in the area of our need for affection/esteem/approval handicaps our ability and freedom to enter into and sustain deep, meaningful relationships with others. Our conscious perception of another person we're closely involved with now may be prejudiced and blinded by the unconscious projection of unresolved issues involving past close relationships. I've seen in my own life that knowing about such relationship projections in theory doesn't prevent one from carrying them out in practice, if one has unresolved issues and memories. When persons we are currently involved with are unconsciously associated or identified with individuals and experiences from past relationships, our projections from the past get superimposed onto the present person. This causes us to feel and behave toward the current person in our life as if he or she were the person from our former unresolved relationships.

These feelings may be positive or negative, depending on the experiences and memories stored in the unconscious. When the previous relationship involved some sort of wounding, betrayal or hurt that's not been fully healed or forgiven, then the projection will contaminate our present relationship with negative feelings and misperceptions of the person with whom we are currently involved. This obviously creates a barrier in our relationship with the present person, preventing us from accurately seeing or being present to her or him in the relationship. Often, when such unconscious relationship projection occurs, we will act out our unresolved feelings toward the previous person on the one with whom we're currently having a relationship. Thus, prior wounding and disappointment may prevent us from being free to enter into or sustain deep, meaningful relationships in the present.

## III

As we've seen, false-self happiness programs related to our basic need for affection/esteem/approval may take expression in various ways. These happiness programs may involve expressions of exaggerated neediness for attention, affection, esteem, or approval from others. Or they may involve egocentric denials and rejection of this basic need on the conscious level. These two basic ways (positive and negative) of responding to unmet needs for affection/esteem/approval in terms of false-self happiness programs draw upon our basic instinctual tendencies toward kindness and cruelty, which are the evolutionary precursors to good and evil in the human soul.

Being "good" to earn rewards of affection/esteem/approval and compulsive people-pleasing behavior patterns are examples of happiness programs motivated by our basic instinctual tendency toward kindness. In these cases, kindness is used not only as an end in itself but as a means of pursuing a hidden agenda. On the other hand, attitudes and behaviors ranging from not caring, being "bad" and "hurting others first" to extreme sadomasochistic perversions and criminal sociopathic tendencies are obvious examples of happiness programs motivated by our instinctual tendency toward cruelty. All of these are unhealthy, the cruelty patterns for obvious reasons and the kindness patterns because, rather than being motivated by kindness as an end in itself, they are motivated by a drive to manipulate others into giving us what we want. This self-centered manipulation typically involves moral/ethical compromises of self-deception as well as the deception of others. Hence, motivated by selfishness and fear, the apparent kindness in people-pleasing, or other seemingly positive affection/esteem/approval happiness programs, is corrupted by mixed motives involving selfishness, manipulation and insincerity on our part.

Hatred (the resentment we feel), lies (self-delusion) and slavery (bondage to emotional happiness programs), our basic criteria of evil, are all present and active in false-self patterns involving affection/esteem/approval motivations and desires. It makes little, if any difference how good our conscious intentions may be. On an unconscious level, we are acting out of childish selfishness while manipulating and using another person in order to get what our happiness program demands.

The reality of the situation is that, in needing to be needed for fear of rejection, etc., we end up betraying our self and our own true needs. Our conscience tries to tell us this and eventually, after the drama fades, we sense with regret that something essential is missing; and we come to see that our interpersonal life and relationships have been a mediocre compromise, or possibly something worse. Whatever exploitation or abuse we may suffer as a "self-sacrificing" people-pleaser, for example, we've brought on our self in our desperate pursuit of attention, acceptance and inordinate affection/esteem/approval.

A major healthy way of pursuing affection/esteem/approval is through intimate personal relationships that are free of childish happiness programs. Such relationships tend to be less superficial and more meaningful than trying to impress others by means of external appearances or symbolic displays of status, prowess, kindness, or accomplishment. We all have a legitimate human need for at least one or two deep personal relationships in our lives. Such healthy relationships evolve from affection/esteem/approval into our higher need for intimacy/belonging. True friendship is shelter for the soul where we may give and receive love with someone we care about who knows us on a deep personal level. This takes us beyond our need for affection/esteem/approval into something far greater.

There comes a point in our human and spiritual life where we outgrow our need for superficial affection/esteem/approval from others; and, beyond that, there comes a point where we outgrow our need for affection/esteem/approval from others altogether. These points of inner growth and freedom come to us in three basic ways: 1) through the inner strength and self-esteem we gain via a few healthy intimate human relationships; 2) through growing into conscious harmony with our conscience; and 3) via intimacy with God. This happens as we receive the grace of affirmation from the divine in our soul. Then, our blossoming spiritual need for intimacy/belonging supersedes our emotional need for affection/esteem/approval.

Those of us who have not yet evolved to such heights in harmony with the divine are bound to remain subject, to some degree, to the four Fruits of the Fall and our basic need for affection/esteem/approval. For most of us, this is an essential part of our existential reality as we continue our spiritual journey and sojourn in human ground. As events in personal relationships and our outer life combine with the inner workings of grace to reveal us to ourselves, we may humbly discover the extent of our subjection to this basic human need.

## IV

Issues of power/control concern all of us because human life requires us to make choices in relating to others, God and our circumstances; and because we are responsible for how we use whatever power/control we possess. Our ability to make intelligent choices is an essential aspect of personal freedom and power/control. This requires awareness of our feelings and values combined with accurate information regarding what our choices are and what their consequences will likely be. Since we rarely, if ever, know everything regarding our choices, exercising free will in making them also involves elements of trust, faith, and risk, especially when outcomes depend on others who also have free will.

A key area where we exercise power/control is in human relationships. Healthy use of power/control respects the legitimate rights, needs and freedom of others while unhealthy power/control does not. This holds true in relations among both individuals and groups; and it holds true in our relationship to conscience and our deep inner self.

Unhealthy distortions and exaggerations of our need for power/control come about as ways of compensating for experiences of helplessness, powerlessness, fear, frustration, anger, insecurity and abuse. When our need for power/control is distorted into emotional happiness programs, it extends beyond our legitimate needs for personal freedom, orientation and self-determination into the situations and lives of others. That is, rather than simply wanting power/control over our own life and destiny, we feel a need to have it in the lives and destinies of others, as a means to gaining mental security/survival/safety and getting what we want. This includes wanting to have our own way too much which often leads to violating of the liberty and rights of others. Such childish, self-centered attitudes cause disharmony, conflict, inequality, and abuse in human relationships. Happiness programs based on our need for power/control tend to separate us from others, thus intensifying our isolation in human ground.

There are various ways power/control may be exercised on others in both personal and impersonal relationships. For example, when people are kept ignorant and misinformed, it's easier to manipulate and control them. This is a common ploy for influencing human thoughts, feelings, beliefs and behavior. Internally, ignorance of the false self and its happiness programs serves to keep us under their power/control. If we neither understand nor are free to choose what motivates us, then our personal freedom and power/control are significantly less than we may believe they are when acting out our happiness programs.

Power/control may be exerted on people secretly or openly, in public or private. When power/control is exercised secretly, people are not conscious of the fact that they're being influenced or manipulated. Giving false or misleading information (lies), engendering fear or mistrust, and deceiving with false advertising and promises are examples of power/control being used secretly to manipulate or trick people.

When power/control is exercised openly, individuals are conscious of it and may choose to accept or resist the manipulation. Being ordered or forced by someone else to do or not do something, whether for legitimate or illegitimate reasons, is an obvious example of power/control being exercised openly. Public manifestations of power/control are done in front of other people and may involve social humiliation and abuse.

Individuals motivated by power/control happiness programs may work themselves into various positions of authority, trust, responsibility and leadership, both to impress others and in pursuit of emotional happiness agendas, e.g., for security, esteem or power/control. At times, individuals may seek inordinate power/control to compensate for low self-esteem. The drive to have more power/control than legitimately needed may be unconsciously associated with security ("Nobody can hurt me"), freedom ("I can do what I want"), and independence ("I don't need anybody") on physical, emotional, mental, psychic, social, and spiritual levels.

In addition to feeling safe, free, and independent, there's a certain seductive pleasure and energy-rush that come from possessing undue amounts of power/control, which can be intoxicating for the false self as ego-inflation fills one with confidence and pride. One begins to feel invincible and worries are banished. Such pleasurable feelings of security and strength may be quite alluring and addicting for the false self, especially when desiring compensation for inner feelings of uncertainty, insecurity, or weakness. Feelings of exaggerated self-importance and exercising authority to the point of being dictatorial often accompany childish, self-centered egos feeding off of inordinate power/control. The outrageous behavior, hubris, and overconfidence that often blind such people typically lead to their downfall, as well as to their inability to understand or empathize with the hardships and suffering others. History and current events are replete with sad examples of this in all areas of human life.

## V

It's been wisely said, "Domination has no place in love."[1] This important insight points to the fact that relying on any form of power/control as our basic modus operandi in close personal relationships tends to undermine those relationships. Hiding behind the masks, manipulations, and one-upmanship of power/control alienates us from others and sabotages any potential for deep, meaningful intimacy in personal relationships.

There are varying degrees to which individuals may rely on exercising power/control for ego-gratification, security, or domination in their relationships. Perhaps we all do this to some extent at one time or another. If so, then our need for healthy relationships is to admit this and work to outgrow it. When misuse of power/control is taken to extremes, we tend to treat our partners not as persons of intrinsic worth but more as objects to be manipulated, exploited, and used for our own gratification and pleasure. Such relationships are dehumanizing, perverse and are liable to contain sadomasochistic elements.

The power/control philosophy of our false self tells us that life is all about competition, winning at any cost, conquering, and dominating. This philosophy allows for moral/ethical compromises and assumes that power/control is what those in the know are all after. Charles Darwin's erroneous "survival-of-the-fittest" theory is a friend to this self-centered power/control philosophy. In opposition to cutthroat power/control and social Darwinism, the case has been convincingly made in both biology and psychology that absolute competition is inimical to physical survival and evolutionary progress for living organisms, especially the human species.[2] The successful alternative to ruthless competition is cooperation. Competition has an obvious place and function in life, but when carried too far by humans, it falls into the destructive ways of cruelty, perversion, and evil for evil's sake.

Our beliefs are our practical map of reality and key to power/control in our lives. If we believe pursuing more and more power/control is necessary for survival, wellbeing, and happiness, then this becomes a primary value and goal. Whenever power is worshipped as an end in itself, moral/ethical infractions and dehumanizing, evil consequences are liable to follow.

Even if we attain the power/control we desire, which rarely happens and, when we do, it's never enough, then in time we'll lose it under the specter of death/change as we age and experience physical/mental decline. If we fail to attain it, which usually happens, then we will feel frustrated and may be reduced to pursuing a semblance of the power/control we want through petty substitutes and compensations. In either case, the end results are not happy because the spiritual poverty of alienation from God, others and our true self remains as long as we give priority to our false self's power/control happiness programs and philosophy.

## VI

The basic pathology of the false self is a misdirection of sex/desire in our soul that amounts to wanting the wrong things or too much of the right things. Our false self's happiness programs are misguided personal agendas that we consciously or unconsciously believe will meet our needs, bring us happiness and fulfill our purpose in our life. These childish compulsions are the idols of ego, gods of the false self that can never deliver on their hopes and promises.

Whenever our false-self happiness programs are frustrated, we fall subject to various afflictive emotions that arise in response. These afflictive emotions tend to dominate our consciousness and outlook on life. For example, when we are carried away by anger, the whole world seems angry, full of hostility, resentment, and hatred. It happens when we are frightened or depressed and the world we live in becomes threatening or gloomy. And so it goes, wherever we go, there we are because we all have a natural unconscious tendency to project what's going on inside us onto the people and world around us.

We see the world through the eyes of our present attitudes and desires, and these are shaped by what we believe and how we feel inside. What we're feeling inside is what motivates us to action, whether for good or for ill. When we are happy and content, then our world and the people in it appear more happy, harmonious, and agreeable, and we tend to express goodwill toward others. When we're at peace, then our subjective attitude toward others and the outer world becomes peaceful too.

On top of the sad fact that our false self's unrealistic happiness programs do not address our soul's true needs and thus cannot possibly work, they also carry dangerous risks involving self-sabotaging good/evil choices and moral/ethical compromises we're liable to make in pursuing them. If we come to rely on negative choices and moral/ethical compromises for pursuing self-centered desires, this inevitably corrupts and retards our character development. With repeated use, negative choices and moral/ethical compromises develop into unconscious habit patterns that come to define our character and run our life, strengthening our false self, sabotaging our human relationships, coloring our worldview and derailing our spiritual progress. These are the inevitable consequences of giving top priority to our emotional programs for happiness rather than to our higher human and spiritual values.

It's important to understand that our happiness programs do not exist in isolation from each other, though each is essentially a self-centered drive for some particular form of compensation. The unique combination of happiness programs in each person forms a single self-contained system. Taken altogether, our particular set of conscious and unconscious happiness programs is what energizes and motivates one's unique false-self system. Often these happiness agendas complement one another and work together for common goals. In other cases, however, particular happiness programs may conflict and work against each other, creating division and disharmony within the false self.

# 10

## Intimacy/Belonging and Happiness Programs

I

Intimacy/belonging, an outer social and inner spiritual need, is our deepest feeling need for connection and relatedness to others, our self and to God. When closeness evokes caring, and caring closeness, intimacy/belonging and love grow in and out of one another. In the best of human and divine relationships, growing intimacy and love create a sense of belonging, togetherness, and unity, filling the hole in our soul with meaning and preciousness.

As our need for love, to know and be known, intimacy/belonging is our highest evolved need connecting our human ground to our spiritual ground. Hence, intimacy/belonging in relation to God and our closest human friendships is also a potential means to healing our soul's emotional wounds. Unfortunately, however, the ways in which we grasp and relate to intimacy/belonging do not always lead us into the blessings of love and our spiritual ground, especially when unconscious projections, emotional happiness programs, and afflictive emotions get in the way.

In this chapter, we focus on the relationship between intimacy/belonging and happiness programs in terms of our quest for love in close personal relationships and in relation to the divine. The broader social and cultural dimensions of intimacy/belonging are discussed in the following two chapters concerning cultural conditioning and human identity. We experience intimacy/belonging in relation to whom or whatever we feel close to, believe in, desire or identify with. This may be, for example, persons, places or things, like a belief system.

Wherever we care and are emotionally invested, intimacy/belonging is present in one form or another because where we care is where we feel close and connected, or desire closeness and connection. Hence, experiences of intimacy, whether real or imagined, create feelings of longing and belonging. Our personal desires hold places of high esteem on our inner intimacy/belonging scale. We feel close to our desires because they are invested with the energy of our heart's treasure. Relationships that are important to us are among our most cherished desires, especially when we feel we may get what we deeply want and need in those relationships. These include our relationships to self, special others and the divine.

Our emotional programs for happiness are also among our most cherished desires, since we believe that satisfying these programs will give us what we want and need to be complete. Happiness programs related to personal relationships and our needs for affection/esteem/approval and intimacy/belonging are of particular significance. Strong feelings of intimacy and desire in relation to another person create a magnetic point of focus in the soul that tends to bring up into consciousness contents involving our happiness programs and past intimate relationships.

Some experiences of intimacy/belonging in close relationships can activate happiness programs and afflictive emotions in us that are blind attempts to compensate for unhealed wounds involving our basic needs and past relationships. We never really know how much emotional baggage we're carrying in our unconscious. It often requires some precipitating event in a current relationship to bring this baggage up into consciousness.

When this happens, we are given an opportunity for new self-knowledge, emotional healing and inner growth, if we can honestly see the situation, take responsibility for our state of consciousness and humbly accept the truth of our emotional baggage and immaturity. Healing can happen in such situations only when we're able to forgive fully the other person(s) and our self for the emotional damage and pain involved. Doing these things is a challenge because our false self always prefers to act out of its afflictive emotions and childish demands, holding grudges and blaming the other person, rather than taking personal responsibility.

Coming to a new point of self-discovery regarding our false self often involves going through afflictive emotions that are activated when happiness programs are frustrated. The overreactions of afflictive emotions always indicate that a happiness program is frustrated. If we buy into afflictive emotions, feeling they're justified or acting them out, then our current relationship suffers and we miss an opportunity for emotional healing and inner growth. Identifying with our afflictive emotions as totally legitimate and justified simply reinforces and strengthens our false self by feeding more energy and power into its happiness programs and afflictive emotions. Self-righteousness in afflictive emotions always blinds us to seeing a situation or relationship objectively, as it really is. To overcome or heal such blindness, we need to compassionately view the situation from the other person's point of view, take responsibility for our emotional reactivity, and we need truly to forgive the other and our self.

## II

Satisfying our deep need for intimacy/belonging is the one thing that can give us deep inner happiness and fill in the hole in our soul. This is something we all sense subconsciously if not consciously. Hence, the compelling, irresistible attraction of intimacy/belonging and whatever symbolizes it for us. We feel the attraction of intimacy/belonging wherever we perceive its hope or pursue its promise; for example, through a quest for deep meaning and purpose, through intimate relationships, or in our quest for God and the true self.

We sense this but, paradoxically, at the same time we often fear intimacy/belonging, experiencing a kind of approach-avoidance conflict in relation to it. Why is this? We certainly don't fear all intimacy/belonging. The kind of intimacy/belonging we may fear is that which we feel will curtail our freedom or expose us to things in our self that we do not want to face or may not be ready to face. Deep intimacy with another person inevitably exposes us, making us vulnerable to her or him and to our own unconscious. Welcoming this requires a high level of trust in both the other person and our self. The same holds true in our relationship with God, who we should know is worthy of complete trust. If we have unresolved issues we're unwilling to face, or if we've been hurt in the past in a close relationship, it may be difficult for us to let our self go emotionally and trust another person. As the saying goes, "once burned, twice shy." Hence, we may fear intimacy/belonging in a close relationship while also desiring it to meet our soul's need for intimacy/belonging.

Authentic intimacy/belonging has the power to reveal the truth of our soul to us and to others. This includes the shadow-self or dark side of our personality as well as our loving true self. Deep experiences of intimacy/belonging in close relationships, or in relation to God, tend to unmask our false self and dark side in addition to revealing our true self or inner core of goodness. Thus, in bringing more of our whole self to the fore, including the dark side, deep experiences of intimacy/belonging create a path to what Thomas Keating calls "the unloading of the unconscious."[1] Fully engaged intimacy has the power to bring up both the best and the worst in us. This is true in both close human relationships and in our relationship to God, where the divine action of love exposes us to our self in order to heal us.

What comes up into consciousness for us when the unconscious unloads and our inner darkness is brought to light? Some typical examples include our soul's unfinished business with pending personal issues involving unresolved experiences, unhealed relationships, afflictive emotions and our childish programs for happiness. When our inner darkness surfaces, it usually does not do so in a way that we can see it objectively, as detached observers. Instead, it typically comes up in the form of afflictive emotions, negative imaginings, fears, and projections that possess our consciousness, distorting our perceptions of self, others and our life drama. When we are unable to recognize them for what they truly are, these subjectively real illusions and other expressions of unresolved issues become primary obstacles to our inner freedom, peace of mind and ability to grow as human beings and spiritual beings. They tend to hold us back and may sabotage our most important relationships to self, others and God.

Personal involvement in an intimate, caring relationship is said to function like a lightning rod for storms of unresolved experiences, feelings, and relationships in our soul's emotional energy-field, drawing in whatever pending issues we have that need healing and closure.[2] In addition to bringing us much happiness and joy, intimacy/belonging in close relationships increases our sensitivity and vulnerability to emotional-happiness-program frustration and afflictive emotions, opening us to possible misery and heartbreak while giving us opportunities to face unresolved issues. When intimacy magnifies sensitivity and emotional issues in the soul, it requires only some precipitating event and corresponding symbolism to activate the projection of an unresolved relationship, issue, or afflictive emotion into consciousness. This may involve our wounded need for affection/esteem/approval.

When our basic need for affection/esteem/approval is wounded, our need for intimacy/belonging is also wounded, as the one need grows out of the other. We cannot freely or fully pursue our need for intimacy/belonging as long as our affection/esteem/approval need remains wounded. Healing our emotional wounds via letting-go, forgiveness and inner renewal are required before we may outgrow our subjection to unmet affection/esteem/approval needs.

The painful memories of unhealed emotional wounds are carried forward inside us. This hidden inner baggage often limits our ability to trust and our willingness to open and be vulnerable to another person, for fear of exposing and re-experiencing our buried wounds. When there is fear regarding intimacy in the soul, we are liable to seek instead a shallow substitute or pseudo-intimacy in our close relationships or spiritual life. Pseudo-intimacy may take various forms, ranging from the shallow and superficial to the mean and perverse. Pseudo-intimacy is often one-sided and is mostly an intimacy we imagine or pretend exists. We might call it "fantasyland intimacy." Such intimacy always fails to satisfy because it cannot give us any real deep connection with another person or the love we need. Real intimacy unmasks us, makes us vulnerable, and shows the other (and our self) more of our whole self. Pseudo-intimacy, on the other hand, is an intimacy of false-self happiness programming that unconsciously plays at intimacy while hiding behind predetermined roles and masks. It's a symbolic substitute, surface cover-up and counterfeit imitation of true intimacy.

Intimidated by fear and ego's need to save face, pseudo-intimacy holds back, showing only what it wants to show, sharing only what it dares to share. Inspired by love and trust, authentic intimacy brings one's whole self to the relationship, revealing strengths and weaknesses, mature and immature parts of our self to the other, the good, the bad, the beautiful and the ugly. Such authentic intimacy becomes appropriate when an interpersonal relationship reaches the level of true friendship (as opposed to friendliness and acquaintanceship). This kind of intimacy is seldom if ever absolute; it can be scary and involves taking risks. Hence, it requires a relationship with the right person and a deep level of mutual empathy, trust, and respect.

In its naked honesty, simplicity, and innocence, true intimacy reveals the soul, confesses the heart, conceals no secrets, but gives the truth of our self to know and be known. This happens in two or three distinct phases: First we idealize the other in an intimate relationship, often projecting our unconscious images of desire, perfection, and happiness onto her or him. This projection causes us to feel close and intimate with the other, though it's actually our own unconscious projection superimposed on the other person to which we are responding. Such experiences can be very moving, inspiring, captivating, obsessing, or, in some cases, madly infatuating, as, for example, when someone falls passionately and blindly in love. In the second phase, we begin to realize that intimate other as the real person he or she actually is. This happens as the truth of hidden flaws and unresolved issues (invoked by the emotional lightning rod of intimacy/belonging) come out into the open. Then we begin to withdraw our idealized projection from the other and are faced with more of the actual reality of her or him as a real person.

We are also faced with more of the reality of our self in relation and response to this unanticipated revelation. The inevitable unmasking activated by shared intimacy shatters the illusions of our idealized hypnotic projections, forcing us to withdraw them back into our self and to begin to see the other more as he or she really is. The disillusionment this brings always creates a crisis or testing point in a close relationship, forcing us to make a "yes" or "no" choice regarding the other person and the relationship. Do we stay or go, accept or reject?

The third phase comes when, after withdrawing our idealistic projections, we choose to accept and love the other person as he or she is now known to be. If we do so, we also gain an opportunity to discover, accept, and love our self on a deeper, more authentic level. This process of growing intimacy/belonging works both ways and requires a mutual effort if it's to evolve forward. It has the potential to take us into a deeper, more committed intimacy and relationship where two may feel truly at home together, with a deep sense of belonging or place.

The back-and-forth process of revealing self to other and other to self tests the sincerity of our heart and, if we say "yes" to one another as we are, makes close personal relationships increasingly real and meaningful. Such consciously committed, fully engaged interpersonal intimacy is a spiritual practice that helps to meet our deep need for intimacy/belonging in human ground. It lets us know we are not alone in this world and that we have someone precious and close to care for who also cares for us.

An important aspect of meaningful intimacy/belonging related to mutual acceptance is the magic of play, fun and laughter, the spontaneous pleasure suddenly found in unexpected coincidences, surprises and acceptance triggered in the moment by ironic or incongruous juxtapositions of thoughts, feelings, actions and events. Humor, play and laughter are natural ways of intimate communication, mutual enjoyment or self-enjoyment. They help to forge the intimate "pleasure bond" of freedom and fondness among individuals and within the self. Play and laughter are ways of confessing and discovering our self anew because they always let something out from inside us; a little silliness and laughing help to keep us from taking our self too seriously. What we play and laugh about always reveals something of what's going on inside us, how we feel, think and what we may take too seriously or not too seriously. The grace of spontaneous play and good humor releases anxiety and stress in the soul, freeing us from fears and other afflictive emotions. It's a return to the innocence and magic of childhood and an essential part of the soul's Lost Paradise.

Such ideal intimacy creates deep bonding and a shared feeling of belonging as its love flows freely into the light of what is now among us, holding us in sacred friendship while filling up the lonely holes in our souls. Authentic interpersonal intimacy/belonging blossoming into growing love is a discovery of Paradise Found, a return to our Lost Paradise. It's a holy dream for which the soul hungers, a dream to realize that attracts us to the hope and promise of intimacy/belonging in close personal relationships of all types. Such intimacy/belonging, where love awakens, is true nourishment for the soul.

Why is this wonderful ideal of intimacy/belonging so rarely discovered or sustained in close personal relationships? Though we may hope for it greatly or glimpse it briefly, it seldom remains on its own, and holding or cultivating it requires much interpersonal work and commitment. Love's magic is so often lost in close personal relationships because there are formidable obstacles in us that oppose the growth of healthy intimacy/belonging. Shyness, fear, unhealed wounds and unresolved emotional issues, false-self happiness programs and afflictive emotions may all get in the way of ideal intimacy/belonging, derailing us in our hoped-for return to the soul's Lost Paradise of intimacy and love.

We may experience glimpses of ideal intimacy/belonging under unique circumstances of meaningful communication, or falling in love; but it's challengingly difficult to sustain such returns to our soul's Lost Paradise. Whatever needs healing has to be healed before we can grow into returning or remaining there unhindered, and there's always the essential, uncertain element of love's mysterious gratuitous grace that may or may not bless a particular relationship. Haunted by insecurities, fears and painful memories, we may be reluctant or even resistant to taking the plunge into vulnerability, intimacy, and full self-disclosure. Therefore, we may withdraw into the less risky compromise of pseudo-intimacy or a surface-intimacy whenever we're unable to enter or remain in the challenging, disarming presence of deep intimacy/belonging where love manifests the truth of our soul.

## III

Lest our distinction between ideal authentic intimacy/belonging and pseudo-intimacy create a false impression, it needs to be said that these contrasting opposites are more abstract extremes than they are actual concrete manifestations in the real world of human relationships. The contrast is drawn to help us distinguish between them. In actual fact, close intimate relationships tend to be relative mixtures of authentic intimacy/belonging and surface pseudo-intimacy. To the degree we sincerely care and honestly share in a close relationship (whether with another person, our self or with God), the intimacy in that relationship is real in spite of any pseudo-intimacy that's present. The vast majority of close personal relationships are changing, relative combinations of real intimacy/belonging and pseudo-intimacy, where we are sincere, hold back, hide, reveal our self, project unconscious contents and are honest or not.

Until our soul is fully healed, its wounds forgiven and our true self awakened, we are all bound to project our unconscious contents onto others to some extent whenever the right conditions arise. It is through interacting with its unconscious contents that the soul tries to resolve pending issues and heal itself. When projecting is done unconsciously, there's scant chance for resolution and healing to take place because we're under the spell of an illusion and don't know what's really going on. It's possible in theory for healing to take place, given the appropriate symbolic interactions among consciousness, the unconscious and our life drama, but highly unlikely. Such seemingly accidental healing by love, grace, and fortunate coincidence would be nothing short of miraculous.

When projections are activated in close relationships, they are evoked into consciousness by the requisite combination of person, circumstances, and imagery that possess the power to call them forth from the unconscious. Another important factor involved here is the urgency our soul has to manifest and work through its unconscious contents expressed in the projection. The desires contained in emotional happiness programs are one important source of unconscious projections. The blockages created by unhealed relationships, wounds, afflictive emotions and other unresolved issues are another. Often these two general sources of unconscious projections are tied together. That is, emotional happiness programs are not only desires that distort and exaggerate our basic instinctual needs, but they are also attempts to compensate for the felt deprivation, wounding, or abuse of those needs.

The healthy fulfillment of our need for intimacy/belonging in personal relationships is based on living and giving the eternal spiritual values of love, truth, and freedom. This requires honoring the intrinsic worth of others as precious spiritual beings; it challenges us to honesty in our communications and dealings with others. Moreover, giving love, truth and freedom to others requires giving others freedom to make their own decisions and to be whom they choose to be.

We may do this only to the degree we've outgrown our childish selfishness, insecurity and emotional happiness programs of the false-self system. From the false self's perspective, becoming vulnerable to others by giving them love, truth, and freedom is the height of foolishness, madness and impracticality because this places the priority of one's own self-centered agendas at risk. Authentic intimacy/belonging is counterintuitive for the false self.

What would it be like if all our needs were somehow met and we lived an ideal, perfect life in intimacy/belonging? Living freely in the fullness of our true self, we'd have no need of unconscious projections or programs for happiness. The course of our life and growth in human and spiritual ground would be marked by the following general pattern: From the primal intimacy/belonging of our Lost Paradise before physical birth, to the intimacy/belonging of meeting our basic instinctual need for security/survival/safety in our mother's arms and breasts, we would bear the deep imprints of life's kindness and goodness. Our many and varied experiences of sensation/pleasure would continue to affirm the wonder and goodness of life, allowing us to identify with Nature and to feel a part of life and the universe.

In our soul's affective domain, meeting our need for affection/esteem/approval would give us the blessing of emotional wellbeing and security, a treasured sense of love and belonging that subsequently evolves into the richer discovery and fulfillment of our need for intimacy/belonging. The crowning glory of these blessings in our life would be an exhilarating sense of personal and spiritual freedom. This blessed inner freedom of the soul comes through the meeting of our need for intimacy/belonging with the full healthy unfolding of our basic need for power/control in harmony with higher human values, our innate conscience, and the divine plan. This healthy and mature power/control gives us personal freedom and independence in human ground and harmony with our true self and God's will in spiritual ground.

The above summarizes an ideal pattern for our life and growth as human beings and spiritual beings in terms of our basic instinctual needs. Such life and growth would, of course, have to take place within the context of the four Fruits of the Fall. The highest key to this is meeting our basic instinctual need for intimacy/belonging, which brings us into our soul's Lost Paradise of true love in relation to another person or persons in human ground and in relation to God and our true self in spiritual ground (Paradise Found). A certain minimal meeting of our basic needs for security/survival/safety, sensation/pleasure, affection/esteem/approval and power/control is prerequisite to the discovery, pursuit and fulfillment of our higher need for intimacy/belonging.

When, as is generally the case, our basic instinctual needs for security/survival/safety through power/control are wounded or not adequately met, it is not possible for us to follow freely such an ideal pattern of life and growth as outlined above. Our fate in fallen human ground is to suffer emotional wounding and fall prey to emotional happiness programs, unconscious projections and the misguided pursuits of our false self. Given this state of affairs, and our subjection to the Fruits of the Fall, it is necessary for us to struggle to overcome what opposes us, choose our true values and become our true self. Though we may not be able to do this on our own, divine help is always available to us. We need only ask for the help, consent to our transformation, and do our part by cooperating with the process.

## IV

Intimacy may be shared on all levels of our being: physical, vital, emotional, mental, psychic, social, and spiritual. Two lovers innocently enjoying their nakedness in the Garden of Paradise is symbolic of all authentic intimacy/belonging, where masks of pretense are dropped. Physical intimacy symbolizes deep interpersonal intimacy, self-disclosure, and mutual sharing where nothing is hidden. We do well to remember, however, that physical nudity, by itself, is obviously no guarantee of intimacy on any level beyond the temporary physical. Ideal human sexual symbolism is the concrete imagery of intimacy/belonging reflected in the human body and in the energy exchanges of close personal relationships. This symbolic imagery of attraction, communion and union moves and integrates our consciousness from earthy levels of human ground on up into sublime levels in spiritual ground. Hence, sexual symbolism is written in our soul as intuitive ideal and goal; that is, as the spiritual goal of communion and union with non-created Reality, our immortal Paradise Found.

Attraction evokes intimacy and intimacy leads to belonging, to knowing and being known. Feelings of true belonging, to another, others or to the divine deep within, take us out of our isolated separate-self sense. Overcoming our existential aloneness/incompleteness is an essential function of our need for intimacy/belonging. Toward this end, we have our outer unions of intimacy/belonging below in human ground and relationships, and we have our inner unions of intimacy/belonging above in spiritual ground with our deep inner self and God.

All outer unions and relationships below in human ground are temporary expressions of the inner ideal of intimacy/belonging in spiritual ground. True and lasting intimacy/belonging is the inner union that takes place with our divine true self in spiritual ground. These two types of communion and union (inner and outer) may complement each other in time, but the inner union and love in our soul's spiritual ground are what endure beyond time. At best, outer unions of intimacy/belonging in human ground are temporary expressions of the inner intimacy/belonging with our divine true self in spiritual ground.

This is the key point to permanently meeting our spiritual need for intimacy/belonging. It may happen only in spiritual ground, in relation to the divine. The ideal sexual union is that which takes place within the soul as all its masculine and feminine energies evolve into loving harmony and, in communion with divine grace, join together to create the ideal perfect intimacy/belonging in spiritual ground (Paradise Found). This is the mystical marriage where, in Christian Tradition, the soul becomes the bride of Christ, the only begotten Son of God abiding forever in our true center of being. Christ is ultimate intimacy/belonging, the living perfection and fulfillment of universal love dwelling in the deepest center and heart of every soul in created reality.

## V

Love brings forth the truth of our soul that we may know our self and be healed. In brings forth all truth in us, the dark and the light, that we may be reconciled and united in our true self with others and the divine. Love inspires and reveals, drawing the soul's contents into its center, so we may become whole in its healing light. By invoking love, authentic intimacy functions as a lightning rod for storms in our soul's emotional energy-field. Intimacy is related to love and truth, since by way of authentic intimacy we come to know the truth of one another and of our selves, and through this truth we grow into deeper love in Christ.

Love is the divine presence and action alive in our soul. Love reveals us to ourselves and to one another. As this revelatory process advances, love reveals to us the divine presence within us and it reveals us in the divine presence. As it is written, "God is love," (1 John 4:8). The intimacy/belonging of love evolving to perfection in us is our way to growing identification with, participation in and belonging to the divine love, truth, and freedom of non-created Reality (Paradise Found). Growing and deepening intimacy/belonging is the path to love and union on all levels of creation and beyond. Our intimacy with everything pre-exists in God and in the deepest center of our soul.

Love connects and unites us to the divine presence in others and in our self. The key to union with the divine is found and used most effectively by imitating the divine in how we relate to creation, others and our self; that is, by giving love, truth and freedom to whatever degree we are able. Inner union with the divine gives us completion and fulfillment in our self. This growing inner completion gradually frees us from addiction and enslavement to all conscious and unconscious happiness programs of our false self. We grow in intimacy/belonging with divine love, truth and freedom via increasing participation and identification with our true divine self in spiritual ground and Ultimate Mystery.

We all have the Feminine and Masculine Principles of creation within us. Every soul is created and energized by the interactions of these principles magnified in its energy-field. If we can harmoniously unite the feminine and masculine energies of our being within us in love on all levels, then we will be complete in our self. This is the true mystical marriage and liberation of the soul joining consciously to its Source in spiritual ground (Paradise Found).

We may try to achieve this inner union outwardly, through intimate human relationships, and we may temporarily experience it here, since the dramatic symbolism of what's happening in our outer life correlates directly to what is simultaneously happening in our soul's inner life. But it is only through an abiding inner union of our soul's feminine and masculine energies that we may attain, by God's grace, the freedom of lasting fulfillment and completion in our self. No adequate symbolic substitute for this abiding inner spiritual union may be found in our outer human-ground life and drama. Yet actions and events in our outer relationships may indeed help us to achieve it; for as we relate to the feminine and masculine in the outer world, so do we affect their corresponding energies within us, and vice versa.

In our quest for love in this life, we mostly play at intimacy. When blessed by divine grace, we actually find it. All the true love and intimacy we give and receive are sheer gift, and, we are gifted so that we may give in return. Nothing is more intimate than love itself, the intimacy/belonging of communion, union, and oneness. It is the fullness of familiarity and preciousness in the deepest sense. The intimacy of love reveals the whole truth of our soul, as it brings together all the disparate parts of our being into its light of integrating oneness. This is the spontaneous work of divine action in us. It's the work of that mysterious, intimate super-conscious presence in which our soul and all created reality are rooted, grounded, and contained. Love reveals ultimate truth and this truth gives full freedom to the soul.

# 11

## IDENTITY QUEST AND CULTURAL CONDITIONING

I

Asking questions and seeking answers always starts us on a quest. For each of us, our personal identity quest, whether conscious or unconscious, is an ongoing, evolving process of inner exploration and self-discovery. It's our private search to know our self and find out who we truly are. Certain fundamental questions are central to each person's identity quest. Some common examples are: Who am I? What am I? What is the meaning or purpose of my life?

These perennial questions preexist and are implied by the nature of our life in human ground. They arise in consciousness if and when we begin to seriously reflect on our needs, desires and life as human beings and spiritual beings. Basic self-awareness, experiences in human life and relationships, and foreknowledge of eventual physical death all tend to give rise to curiosity, concern and wonder; and these in turn give rise to life's basic existential questions: Who am I? What am I? What is the meaning or purpose of my life? The society we are born into and its cultural/religious conditioning supply us with various prefabricated, partial answers to these questions, answers that are given us before we can under-stand or begin to ask these questions in a conscious, heartfelt way.

Answers to life's basic existential questions are supplied by cul-tural conditioning from childhood on, shaping our sense of personal identity and orientation to life within the context of our immedi-ate environment and important relationships. It starts when we are given a name. We identify with our immediate family, culture and society, adopting their values, ways and beliefs as our own in order to fit in and get our basic needs met. In doing so, we become part of a shared group-identity where certain essential beliefs, values, goals and a consensus view of reality are held in common. This serves to ground us in our world.

From early on, we internalize and are effectively programmed with the beliefs, values, worldview and so forth of our cultural conditioning, which has both positive, life-affirming qualities and negative limitations and prejudices. Our cultural conditioning gives us a needed sense of orientation to life and provides us with some easy, ready-made answers to our identity quest. It affects us on many levels, helps to shape our sense of self, and plays a key role in determining our individual psychology, consciousness and behavior patterns throughout life, affecting both our attitudes and desires.

In giving us ready-made answers to our identity quest, cultural conditioning may tell us that we are "what we have" or "what we do." For example, cultural conditioning may inform us that we are our physical body, emotions, intellect, abilities, and skills, relationships, the roles we play, our profession, etc. These things are like the clothes we wear on our physical body, which our core inner self may put on or take off. They are important and necessary things that we have, use or do, but they are not who we ultimately are as spiritual beings. For example, as any actor knows or should know, we are not the roles we play in human life. Our various roles are subject to change and express our surface outer self or personality. How we play these roles, however, may express our creativity and reveal something of our deeper inner self, especially when we are fully engaged in playing them.

At most, the various things that we have and do, e.g., our physical body, emotions, intellect and roles in life, are living expressions of who we are. They form what we might call our transitory "peripheral identity," which is whom we appear to be to others and our self. The things we have and do are not our core identity, which is our enduring inner identity as a spiritual being. Our true inner-self-identity precedes and transcends cultural conditioning and our life in human ground. This is a profound and important point. Our true self as a spiritual being is what we are ultimately seeking when we ask deep in our heart, "Who am I?"

We do not become capable of truly comprehending or asking life's basic existential questions until our intellect and self-consciousness evolve from adolescence into adulthood; that is, until we become able, to some extent, to think independently for our self. Who we are as unique individuals is a question whose answer continually changes throughout life as we gather new experiences, defining and redefining whom we are via our choices and actions. What we desire and believe, and what we do and do not do play key roles in defining who and what we are or think we are as unique human beings.

What we are as individual human beings is answered first by the given raw material of our evolutionary origins and heritage, and by our innate possibilities as human and spiritual beings subject to basic instinctual needs and the Fruits of the Fall. Second, what we are is answered by the influences of cultural conditioning and by what we actually do with our inherent possibilities and gifts throughout life, given the particular circumstances, experiences, and relationships available to us. Hence, what we become as unique human and spiritual beings depends on the following: 1) our given inner and outer existential circumstances, 2) who and what come to us in life. And 3), most importantly, how we respond to these things and what we do with our inherent potentials and gifts.

The third basic existential question concerning our life's meaning and purpose is answered for each of us by what we genuinely care about. What we value and who we care about provide key answers to the ongoing question of our identity quest because we are identified with our caring. How cultural conditioning educates us obviously influences what or whom we are liable to value and care about.

For caring options in life's game, we have two basic kinds of choice. On the one hand, there is a divine plan for created reality's evolution and perfection in which we are invited to participate. This option represents the path of healthy character development, spiritual growth and inner awakening. On the other hand, we are also free to set our own agendas and pursue our own desires and programs for happiness as we choose. These are the broad alternatives available to us. Most of us try them both at different times. What we choose to care about depends on what we're aware of or believe in to care about. From this fact we may see the practical importance of cultural conditioning, our inner education, and self-knowledge.

So the meaning and purpose of our life is essentially a matter of what's most important to us, what we place value in and invest with the energy of our heart's preciousness; and then what we do about it. What we care about may be a person, place, thing, or some combination thereof. Consequently, life's meaning and purpose may be very different for different people. How our culture educates us strongly influences what life's meaning and purpose are for us.

Cultural conditioning does this by teaching us 1) what our choices are and 2) which choices are worthy to be esteemed as goals of our longing and desire. Cultural conditioning also teaches us, by word and by example, how to go about attaining our goals and getting what we want. Sometimes there are mixed messages in cultural conditioning involving good/evil choices regarding how to reach our goals or get what we want. In doing all of this, cultural conditioning effectively predetermines many of our important choices, though we are always free, at least potentially, to choose other ways of belief and action.

Since love is the highest value of meaning and preciousness in human and spiritual ground, it is the combination of how we love and what we love that ultimately determines the practical meaning and purpose of life for each of us. That is, the relative qualities of how we love and what or whom we love combine to create the corresponding qualities of meaning, value, and purpose we experience in life. In addition, these are all subject to change as we discover new ideals and loves. Our formative early-life experiences of meaning and purpose touch us most deeply and are central to our evolving sense of personal identity and value, forming vital strands and defining themes in our personal story.

The various goals we pursue are expressions of what we value and care about. Hence, this process may add precious meaning to our life, depending on what we pursue and how we pursue it. For a person to accomplish anything worthwhile requires time, effort, patience and motivation to keep going until the goal is reached. All of this, and the hard work it requires, helps us to grow up, builds individual character, strengthens our sense of identity, and contributes to spiritual growth, if it's done in ways that express the higher human and spiritual values of our innate conscience.

What dedication, self-discipline, honest effort, and so forth accomplish in us on the spiritual level, i.e., our inner character development, is far more important and longer lasting than all the temporary goals and accomplishments we may pursue and achieve on the human ground level. This is because the inner strength and nobility of character that come from pursuing our temporary goals with integrity and honor serve to nourish our life in spiritual ground. Moreover, this has eternal value for the soul beyond the passing movements of death/change affecting our ephemeral life and accomplishments in human ground.

## II

Cultural conditioning is a powerful formative process that takes place in every society where individual members internalize and identify with the various characteristics that define their society. These include such outwardly noticeable things as styles of dress, sports, hobbies, entertainment, vocations, diet, speech and body language. Spoken language is a key factor in cultural conditioning because it influences how we think, feel, view the world, express our self and understand one another. Language also programs us, affecting how we treat one another. Internally, cultural conditioning shapes our attitudes, beliefs, values, tastes, opinions, desires and consciousness. It gives us collective myths and stories with which to identify, a sense of history and tradition, as well as particular ways of interpreting life. All this, and sharing it with others, serves to ground us in our unique world.

Sharing culturally conditioned attitudes, beliefs and so forth with others allows us to understand one another to some degree and to feel we belong to a common group. This helps to meet our needs for affection/esteem/approval and intimacy/belonging on the social level. However, in identifying too closely with our culture, we may take the "truths" of its historical mythos and cultural conditioning as absolute and thus lose the capacity to separate our self from them and view them objectively. Then we tend to see the world and everything in it through the eyes of our cultural conditioning. This has been true since ancient times.

In the twentieth century, the social sciences of psychology, anthropology, and sociology helped to remove some of our cultural blinders by performing an important and valuable service to our growing understanding of cultural conditioning and human nature. They did this by studying their subject matter objectively, from both outside and inside the system, using perspectives of critical analysis, cross-cultural comparisons and various humanly constructed ideas, theories and beliefs. This research has allowed social scientists to discover many aspects of what human individuals and societies have in common as well as where they differ. It has given us enlightening new views of the reality of existence in human ground and of what human life requires on all levels (physical, vital, emotional, mental psychic, social and spiritual) to function and thrive.

The idea of cultural conditioning, as we may appreciate it today, is somewhat revolutionary in comparison to how the contents of cultural conditioning were automatically and unconsciously viewed and accepted as true and valid in the past. Before the twentieth century, many human societies and groups of people lived in relative isolation from one another. In taking their own particular traditions and cultural conditioning as absolute, they unquestioningly accepted their own humanly created worldviews, religious beliefs, superstitions, cultural mores, customs, values and so forth to be correct and true— sometimes holding them to be divinely inspired and mandated. In other words, their perceptions of reality were culturally conditioned, limited and predetermined to an extreme degree. Such cultural conditioning functions as a kind of blinder or filter placed over consciousness, prejudicing and censoring awareness of what is or may be. This provides a kind of safe, secure container for human consciousness but severely restricts the latitude of its viewpoint.

In earlier times, as in the present, the cultural conditioning and traditions of other groups that differed from one's own were often judged to be inferior, ridiculous, mistaken, or downright evil. There was, as there is today, competition among rival worldviews. Contacts between differing groups tended to change them and often one group sought to forcefully dominate, exploit, control and sometimes enslave another. The cultural conditioning of one group (values, beliefs, etc.) was sometimes imposed, forcefully or otherwise, on other groups with different cultural conditioning. Some dramatic and brutal examples of this occurred between the sixteenth and twentieth centuries with the European-Christian expansion and invasions of Africa and the New World, e.g., the human slave trade and violent takeover of the Americas. Those sanctioning and carrying out these nefarious activities did so primarily for economic gain and nationalistic reasons, labeling their human prey as uncivilized savages and justifying their abusive actions with claims of cultural, religious, and racial superiority.

My stated evaluation of these activities as "nefarious" here is, of course, a reflection of my own human values and cultural conditioning. No doubt, those who sanctioned and did these things viewed them quite differently from the perspectives of their own priorities, values, and cultural conditioning. Otherwise, how could they have done them?[1]

In smaller societies, cultural conditioning is pretty much the same for everybody. In larger societies, there are differing strains of cultural conditioning among subgroups within the overall general group, e.g., cultural diversity within the United States of America. In every society, there is a social contract between the individual and the group. This contract requires the individual to conform to certain expectations and demands of the group. In return, he or she receives whatever real or imaginary benefits the group has to offer. These benefits may be of a social, political, economic, sexual, religious, or personal nature.

Theoretically, and to some degree practically, the benefits of conforming to cultural conditioning involve helping individuals meet their basic instinctual needs for security/survival/safety, sensation/pleasure, affection/esteem/approval, power/control and intimacy/belonging. This is the implicit hope and promise of the human herd instinct in every society. Our psychological reliance and dependency on the group and its members to help us get our needs met are what make the social/psychological contract of cultural conditioning so very strong and binding.

The programming of cultural conditioning shapes our consciousness and behavior as we strive to become accepted members of our group. The group offers us a shared cultural identity and promises to help meet our needs. Society is perceived as powerful and able to give us the affection/esteem/approval, security/survival/safety and so forth that we need, along with a share in its collective power. These impressions are especially strong in early life when we rely most heavily upon others to meet our needs, looking to the world around us and to older role models to show us how to fit in, get on and become successful members of society.

Cultural conditioning and social conformity function both openly and secretly to form the binding agreement between the individual and society. The deal works like this: to get what the group has to offer, we must conform to what the group expects, requires and demands of us. Buying into cultural conditioning is an essential part of this. Love of our cultural conditioning and intimate identification with the group make it easy to conform, unless or until we run into conflicts in which what we want and what the group wants do not agree. Then we have to make some decisions. We may choose to avoid or ignore the conflict and simply go along with our cultural conditioning and what the group asks of us. We can go against the group's expectations either openly or secretly. Or we may leave the group and strike out on our own, maybe finding or even starting another group. We may be conflicted in our self and try a combination of these things. Good/evil choices and conscience often enter into the mix here.

This basic situation is faced by each person in every society the world over. The path of least resistance is to simply conform and go along with our cultural conditioning and group for better or worse. That's obviously what most people do most of the time. However, situations do arise where individuals refuse and choose not to conform to cultural conditioning and group expectations for various reasons. These reasons may involve good/evil choices and may come from the false self or the true self within these individuals. Moreover, as is often the case, they may come from both the true self and the false self as a kind of mixed motivation. Mixed messages found in cultural conditioning, like "do as I say and not as I do," tend to express something of both the true and false self in those who create or pass on the cultural conditioning.

Like individual human beings, every culture, organization, and group has both a collective true self and false self. This is inevitable because all cultures, organizations, and groups are created and made up by individuals with true and false selves. For this reason, it's not surprising that there is a prevalence of mixed messages, inconsistencies, and contrary motives coexisting in much of our cultural conditioning.

Groups tend to reflect the qualities of their leaders and members, and vice versa. As in individual human relationships, there is often rivalry and competition within and among various groups and cultures of human society. In seeking to meet individual and collective needs for security/survival/safety, sensation/pleasure, etc., individual groups of various sizes may try to dominate, control, exploit, conquer, abuse, or even destroy other groups. Therefore, we have the nonstop lethal legacy of corruption, crime, and war in human history and ongoing events. Whatever individuals are liable to do to one another for better or for worse, groups of individuals may do to one another as well.

Some degree of group identification and conformity to cultural conditioning is healthy and necessary for our inner development, functioning and getting along in society. However, too much dependency and over-identification locks us into a mindset that restricts one's inner freedom and spiritual growth. As mentioned above, collective mindsets sometimes teach us prejudices and intolerance of other groups that differ from our own. This causes considerable conflict, misunderstanding, and misery in human life and relationships. Thus, we may be well adjusted to our group or society; but we're also bound by their errors, prejudices, and limitations. Over-identification and naïve loyalty to cultural conditioning tend to blind us to its limitations and faults while reinforcing our prejudices and false-self system.

To be free, self-determined individuals, we need to become conscious of specific aspects of our cultural conditioning and how they affect us. Then we need to take this awareness inside and engage it in deep reflective meditation. There, in our inner room, we may evaluate whether or not particular aspects of cultural conditioning serve us well and are consistent with the values of our true self, spiritual conscience and the person we intend to be? One essential purpose of the spiritual journey is to free us from the unhealthy limitations of cultural conditioning and our false self. These are to be replaced, as Thomas Keating says, by our true self and the divine way of seeing and doing things.

## Dimensions of the Soul and Basic Instinctual Needs

|  | Physical | Vital | Emotional | Mental | Psychic | Social | Spiritual |
|---|---|---|---|---|---|---|---|
| Security/Survival |  |  |  |  |  |  |  |
| Sensation/Pleasure |  |  |  |  |  |  |  |
| Affection/Esteem |  |  |  |  |  |  |  |
| Power/Control |  |  |  |  |  |  |  |
| Intimacy/Belonging |  |  |  |  |  |  |  |

*The reader is invited to fill in the empty spaces in this table, to determine one's current place in terms of emotional happiness programs and in relation to these variables.*

## 12

## CULTURAL CONDITIONING AND IDENTITY SHIFT

I

Identity is an ultimate degree of intimacy in any relationship, human or divine. In human ground, intimacy evolving into identity means feeling one with some person, place or thing (such as cultural conditioning). In spiritual ground, intimacy evolving into identity means becoming one with our true self and God (this includes God's creation). In both categories of intimacy evolving into identity, our basic needs for human and spiritual intimacy/belonging may be pursued and satisfied (or frustrated). As mentioned earlier, our need for intimacy/belonging is both an outer social need and an inner spiritual need. In connecting us to important social, religious and cultural groups, cultural conditioning plays a key role in addressing the social and human-ground aspects of our need for intimacy/belonging.

Progressive degrees of intimacy are suggested by the following: sharing, feeling close, caring, commitment, deepening knowledge, communion, union, unity, and oneness. These last three—union, unity and oneness—represent progressive stages of finding common identity in a relationship of intimacy/belonging. Entering into shared identity with another being, be it human, subhuman or divine, initiates a process of identity shift in us. Love, initially experienced as attraction, is the soul-force of intimacy. Love, manifested on all levels of our being (physical, vital, emotional, mental, psychic, social and spiritual), is the mysterious force that unites two into one, e.g., knower with the known, lover and beloved, and the soul with its Source.

Intimacy evolving into identity with someone or something means that we are the same as he, she or it in some way, and we co-participate in the being, life and fate of whom or whatever we identify with. This co-participation is a basis of compassion (feeling with another) and of vulnerability in that we are affected by how the person or thing with which we identify feels or is affected. Our vulnerability, of course, also extends to how we are treated and affected by the person, place, or thing with which we identify. Such intimate identity invariably changes us for better or worse as we become, to some degree, the same as that with which we identify.

The intimacy of shared identity and co-participation penetrates our soul, infusing us with new energy and life. The stronger or more complete our identification with him, her, them or it, the more vulnerable and affected we become in our intimacy. This holds true in all our close relationships with self, others and God. It is especially true regarding cultural conditioning, which plays a key role in educating and shaping us into who we are as individual human beings and members of society. Hence, we often tend to feel a strong sense of uncritical gratitude, love, loyalty and attachment to cultural conditioning and its biases.

As a member of our home society, which is an object for intimate fusion of self and other by way of loyalty and identification, we feel a sense of belonging connecting us to something greater, something beyond our separate-self sense. Though risky to our personal independence and freedom, this connection to our home society and culture can be deeply precious to us. It connects us to others in society with whom we may form intimate relationships; and intimate identification with society and culture enlarges our sense of identity while reducing our sense of isolation in human ground. In these ways, intimacy/belonging in relation to cultural conditioning helps us cope with existential aloneness/incompleteness. In fact, intimacy/belonging with our cultural conditioning may function as a substitute for deepening and fulfillment in other relationships.

Cultural conditioning forms some of the most basic contents of our identity as members of a particular society, filling in some of the blanks for us as we ask: Who am I? What am I? What is the meaning or purpose of my life? Cultural conditioning identifies us with a particular racial, ethnic, sexual, national, cultural and religious heritage; all of which contributes to our identity in human ground. By virtue of the good things it gives us, cultural conditioning is precious to us, at least to some degree.

Cultural conditioning is a continuing, ongoing process rooted in our unique heritage and history, manifesting forward through our present activities and immediate experience. Trusting our cultural conditioning gives us a feeling of security, grounding, and wellbeing. It gives us agreement with others around us and seems to make life easier. The contents of cultural conditioning help articulate our sense of individual identity and thus form an intimate, important part of who we are or think we are.

In feeling intimacy/belonging with our culture and group, we don't feel as isolated as we may feel on our own without the group. This is liable to become especially the case if there's a lack of meaningful intimacy/belonging in our private, personal life; that is, in close human relationships, or in our inner life and relationship with God. When such is the case, we may become overly dependent on our culture and group for emotional support and a sense of intimacy/belonging. This usually leads to over-identification with cultural conditioning, which becomes like God for us, since we rely on it for so much; that is, we may over-rely on it for our sense of identity, security, intimacy/belonging, orientation, and meaning in life.

When we over-identify with cultural conditioning, our dedication to it may become extreme or fanatical. If it functions as a basis of our psychological or ontological security, as, for example, with certain religious beliefs, then any challenge to our cultural conditioning is felt as a direct challenge or threat to our security/survival/safety. We may react to such perceived challenges or threats with an irrational "fight or flight" response. Over-dependency on and the intimacy/belonging we feel with cultural conditioning may create naïve loyalty and a kind of dogmatic fundamentalism that blind us to seeing its limitations and dark side.

One way the dark side of cultural conditioning gets expressed is through collective happiness programs that distort and exaggerate our basic instinctual needs. These collective happiness programs are often expressed in relation to other, rival groups as, for example, in obsessions with "national security" or in ambitions to exercise power/control over other groups and nations. Collective false-self happiness programs may also be expressed within the group itself. For example, the group may feed its members' needs for inordinate affection/esteem/approval by telling them they are better than members of other groups and are thus entitled to more human rights and privileges than their inferiors.

Powerful feelings of intimacy/belonging may be awakened in large or small groups when group members identify together as individual parts of a common greater cause or shared destiny. These feelings of shared intimacy/belonging become especially strong, binding and inspiring when members believe the group is dedicated to a particularly noble and righteous cause. The sense of serving a higher purpose appeals to our idealistic tendencies, often inspiring self-sacrifice and feelings of meaning, self-transcendence, and intimacy/belonging. This is true whether the cause served ultimately proves to be good or evil.

## II

A key aspect of cultural conditioning that's closely related to identity quest involves the formation of our outer human conscience. This outer conscience comes to us from external sources of influence, such as parents, culture, and society. Our innate spiritual conscience, on the other hand, pre-exists within us and comes to us from the true center of our soul in spiritual ground. Owing to their different respective places of origin, our outer human conscience and our innate spiritual conscience do not always agree and, at times, are liable to oppose each other in deadly conflict.

The development of our outer human conscience, which programs us to live out our core cultural conditioning, is central to the process of adaptation to our home society. Cultural conditioning may reinforce our tendencies toward both kindness and cruelty. Hence, it seems inevitable for conflicts to arise between our acquired human conscience and our innate spiritual conscience which, being grounded in divine love, truth and freedom for all, opposes all forms of cruelty, deception, hatred and bondage, including non-defensive war.

It's important to realize that we're often unconscious of the fact that our human conscience has been programmed into us. Not knowing this, we may take our human conscience for granted or we may mistakenly identify it with our innate spiritual conscience. Since others in society tend to hold the same moral values and ideas of "right" and "wrong," it's easy to simply accept our culturally conditioned human conscience as valid in all cases without questioning or thinking about it. The tacit assumption here is that whatever our social, cultural or religious conditioning mandates has to be right, true and in harmony with God's plan (if we believe in God), no questions asked. Unfortunately, this isn't always the case, as when human conscience inadvertently serves as justification for false-self agendas and tactics.

To whatever degree society is a reflection of authentic spiritual values, its culturally conditioned human conscience will be in harmony with our innate spiritual conscience. To whatever degree society is not an expression of true spiritual values, its outer human conscience will be in conflict with our inner spiritual conscience. Fallen human nature being what it is, with its individual and collective false selves and their various self-centered programs for happiness, it seems inevitable that our acquired human conscience and our innate spiritual conscience would sometimes clash, urging us to follow contrary directions in moral/ethical decision making. This is an example of the third Fruit of the Fall, good/evil choices, manifesting in human ground.

It's natural and healthy to love our cultural heritage and to identify with its positive life-affirming values and practices. But it's far from healthy to over-identify with cultural conditioning and to ignore its limitations and dark side. Those aspects of cultural conditioning that serve the false self need to be exposed and rejected, if we're to have a healthy, peaceful and sustainable society that's true to higher ideals and values. The alternative to this is the pathological self-destruction of moral/ethical decadence and corruption leading eventually to individual and collective war, disintegration, and death.

Psychological research has confirmed repeatedly that there is a direct causal relationship between morality and mental health. This has to do with the inner spiritual law of the soul. Individuals who live moral lives of honesty, integrity, and kindness to others are consistently found to have peace of mind and good mental health. Conversely, when an individual's dominant personality patterns violate basic moral/ethical principles, the self-deceptions, repressed conscience and rationalizations involved create internal stresses that lead to psychological deterioration and self-destructive tendencies. This holds true for groups as well as individuals. Hence, all cultural conditioning that overtly or covertly permits, encourages, or supports false-self happiness programs and violations of true conscience is essentially pathological and harmful to those affected by it.

The disappointing examples of some of our favorite entertainment celebrities and other public figures, who often serve as role models, embarrassing and disgracing themselves with financial, sexual, substance abuse and other scandals is a conspicuous red flag warning us. It warns us that, contrary to some cultural conditioning, being who those people are and having what they have are not what's required to meet the real needs of a human being for happiness, peace of mind and fulfillment in life. It's neither glamorous nor glorious for a human will to succumb to the self-centered immaturity and demands of false-self happiness programs that prove to be degrading and can't possibly work. Actually, unfortunate rich and famous people who follow false-self happiness programs are inadvertently performing a valuable service for us by showing us what does not work in pursuing human health, happiness and wellbeing.

## III

So what to do about cultural conditioning that reinforces false-self values and happiness programs? The best defense against such cultural conditioning is demonstrating the truth of its healthy alternative. This, of course, calls for overcoming, with God's help, our own false-self tendencies and living out of our true self. Education by example is the best answer and most effective teacher. We may disarm and overcome our outer and inner foes not by fear and violence, but by knowing them as they truly are, showing compassion and, as Gandhi said, by "being the change we want to see in our world."

The healthy alternative to false-self happiness programs needs to be demonstrated by sane, peaceful persons living in harmony with our true self. True sanity is wisdom. Wisdom for a human being involves having deep self-knowledge, i.e., knowledge of our false self and our true self, and it involves understanding how things work in us and in our world. As a consequence of such awareness, a wise person knows what her or his true needs actually are and is grateful to enjoy meeting them. A foolish person, on the other hand, does not know this and mistakenly falls into the trap of pursuing more and more beyond the realm of her or his legitimate needs, believing this to be the way to wellbeing and happiness. The sad results of this error are there to be seen by anyone who pays attention.

A wise person finds peace and satisfaction in pursuing higher spiritual values, self-chosen goals and inner growth that address her or his spiritual needs, once one's legitimate material needs are satisfied. When our basic material needs are met, we then have leisure and liberty to pursue higher, non-material needs and goals, should we choose to do so. Being educated as to the full range of our choices and their likely outcomes is essential to how healthy cultural conditioning ought to serve and empower us.

One problem in today's world is that the educational process of cultural conditioning fails to teach about the false self and its happiness programs. It actually teaches the opposite much of the time while giving mixed messages and lip service to higher ideals and values. Unfortunately, rather than warning us about the false self, our dominant cultural conditioning ignores the wonderful potential of our true self while often glorifying illusions of the false self, marketing materialistic values and products that reinforce emotional happiness programs, as if this were the best life has to offer.

If our formal and informal educational systems taught about the true self and the reality of the false self, with its futile happiness programs, then who would consciously choose to pursue them? When seen for what they truly are, the false self and its happiness programs lose their illusory glamour, glory and appeal. On the surface, our choice between the false and true self appears to be a "no-brainer." However, its practical execution requires the power to know which is which and the inner freedom and strength to choose between them. It requires the wisdom of deep self-knowledge and understanding how things work in us and our world.

The challenge and difficulty here lie in the fact that the causal roots of the false-self system and its happiness programs are not out in the open where we can easily see them. They are hidden in the unconscious depths of our soul, to which we do not have free and ready access. What we do see of the false self are its conscious surface symptoms and its many disguises that we mistake for other things, like our true self. The false self's stronghold is hidden from our sight. Hence, it helps but does not suffice to consciously renounce the false self and its happiness programs, once we're aware of them. Doing so is a definite step forward from conscious ignorance, denial, and unconscious bondage to the false self. But conscious renunciation alone does not change or remove the hidden functioning of the false self in our unconscious, which can adapt to any new roles, goals, situations or relationships into which we enter: hence, our need of divine help from within to effectively remedy the problem.

Fortunately, that divine help is readily available. Each of us is part of the divine consciousness and nothing can be hidden from its presence in our soul. We need to humbly ask for this help, consent to the divine action, and we need to cooperate with the process of interior purification, healing and transformation by doing our part on the conscious level. Doing our part involves cultivating our true self and letting go of habitual attachment to emotional happiness programs when opportunities to do so present themselves. The interior journey of this process underlies the identity shift of our false self gradually evolving into our true self. Its lasting fruit is our growth in true wisdom, freedom and abiding entry into our Paradise Found.

IV

We're born into this life to journey through a maze of identity quest from false self to true self. This is a journey of progressive identity shift, moving us from human ground into spiritual ground. As we move through human ground, our sense of self repeatedly changes. This is a natural consequence of the fact that life is change and all human-ground life is subject to the fruit of death/change. We die to one condition to be born into another, over and over again. This pattern is basic for all life in created reality. So, how does our journey of identity quest begin and progress?

In early life, our sense of identity develops around primary relationships and our basic instinctual needs. Initially, our relationship to mother and our needs for security/survival/safety, affection/esteem/approval and intimacy/belonging are paramount. Infants are primarily physical/emotional beings awakening to life in human ground. Self-centeredness and seeking attention from others in relation to the demands of basic instinctual needs are natural in early life and essential for survival, since infants are dependent on others to meet their needs. From this dependency, a core of egocentric selfishness becomes the basis of individual identity in human ground, even before our separate-self sense comes out and emerges into consciousness. In this and subsequent stages of development, our life is all about "me" and what "I" need or want.

So, the sense of self we develop is relational and connected to meeting our needs for security/survival/safety, affection/esteem/approval and so forth. Our false self's emotional happiness programs related to unmet or frustrated basic needs form its primary "operating program" and are already in place in the unconscious before we develop a solid separate-self identity. Our early sense of self first crystallizes around age six or seven in the form of an abiding separate-self sense. This separate-self sense becomes the ontological center and foundation of our human identity and pre-programmed false-self system.

Our false self is shaped into an organized functioning complex from within by distorted and exaggerated basic instinctual needs (happiness programs), and from without by the educational programming of cultural conditioning, with its human flaws as well as its positive qualities. Our false self is who we come to believe we are as a human being not who we really are as a total spiritual being. Our human identity is changing, impermanent and uncertain. Our spiritual identity, on the other hand, includes our human self but is a larger, deeper and longer lasting identity. Our evolving spiritual identity is our eternal identity co-participating in the oneness of non-created Reality while both including and transcending the limitations and vicissitudes of cultural conditioning and our human personality.

We are destined to live our life in human ground torn between the agendas of our false self and our true self until, through persistent humble efforts and God's grace, we negotiate our identity shift from human ground into spiritual ground. Then we may begin living the life of our true self on a more or less continual basis. While our human personality or false self inclines toward both good and evil, our true self inclines exclusively toward good; that is, toward giving love, truth and freedom to self and others in relation to God.

The spiritual law governing the human soul expresses its inner consistency. This law of inner consistency is such that we inevitably end up treating our self as we treat others, and how we treat others expresses and determines how we treat our self. In other words, we may manifest our true self by being truthful and loving to others only to the extent that we are truthful and loving to our self. Conversely, we may be truthful and loving to our self only to the degree that we are truthful and loving to others. The great identity shift from false self into true self requires a good/evil-choices shift from mixed motivations into consistent higher motivations that are in harmony with our innate conscience and true self. The spiritual discipline of being consistently truthful and loving to self and others will accomplish this identity shift in us without fail, if only we can really practice it.

## V

The difficulty is, of course, that we can't really practice it; that is, at least not all the time. We can't really do it because there are forces active in our soul, unconscious forces beyond our control that prevent us from always being truthful and loving. In this simple fact lies our true challenge and humble understanding that we need divine help to overcome our false self and obstacles. What opposes us so tenaciously is the unconscious motivation of our false self in its shadow aspect. The "shadow" in depth psychology is a Jungian concept.[1] It's a kind of anti-self, so far as our conscious self-image is concerned, composed of those parts of the self we've rejected because they're repulsive and contradict our conscious self-image.

We've rejected these "unacceptable" parts of our self from consciousness, disowned and repressed them into unconsciousness, and are generally in denial about them. These rejected shadow parts belong to our wounded self. Their re-entering consciousness typically engenders fear and the re-experiencing of our wounds. Hence, we tend to resist this. Continuing to reject and deny our wounds only serves to perpetuate them along with the false-self happiness programs and afflictive emotions connected to them.

These unconscious wounds are our pending unresolved issues, experiences and relationships, stored as knots in the energy centers of our instinctual needs. Split-off from consciousness, our shadow-self lives a subterranean life and is often at odds with conscience and our conscious desires. It's this rejected shadow in us that inclines toward negativity, evil and the undermining of our better intentions and wellbeing.

Integrating the shadow or dark side of our personality is prerequisite for negotiating the great identity shift from fallen human ground into resurrected life in spiritual ground. Integrating this dark side means admitting it back into consciousness, listening to it in humility and compassion, learning from it, accepting it as is, reconciling it by acknowledging its legitimate feelings and needs, and then lovingly welcoming its energy and presence into the life of our conscious self. Love heals the shadow. Only then will it change and no longer oppose us.

So, healing our shadow requires consciously acknowledging its truth, the truth of wounded needs and pain that underlie it, and giving it understanding, forgiveness and compassion. Visualization and active imagination may aid in this process. It is an act of giving love, truth and freedom to our self on a deep interior level of intimacy/belonging in relation to God and our inner self. The healing power of forgiveness, for our self and others, ought not to be underestimated. It is an essential part of love's healing power. The inner fruit of integrating our shadow is the creation of deep humility and peace in our soul. Integrating our shadow allows us to have understanding and compassion for the shadow-self in others, instead of unconsciously projecting our shadow onto them and consciously judging, attacking, rejecting or hating them. Forgiveness is an indispensable key to healing the subterranean flaws and wounds of our shadow-self hidden deep in the soul's unconscious recesses.

The practical efficacy of forgiving others who have offended us not only releases them from our ill will and negative projections; forgiveness also safeguards our own inner peace since holding resentment and harboring grudges poisons us with the negativity of toxic afflictive emotions. This in turn serves to reinforce our false self and to empower its malefic shadow aspect. Just as habitually lying beclouds our clarity of mind and makes us stupid (as we come to believe our own lies), so does failure to forgive tend to separate us from our pure loving heart as we hold on to the pain of hurts, consciously or unconsciously harboring resentment, anger and desire for revenge in our soul.[2]

In our identity quest, admitting the shadow or dark side into consciousness, accepting and integrating it into the wholeness of self, is the only way to overcome the unconscious cruel, perverse and evil tendencies in our soul. We cannot embrace or integrate the truth of our life by running away from it. Befriending and integrating the shadow is an expression of kindness toward our self. It's a manifestation of love, truth and freedom in the soul that heals and transforms our dark side by welcoming this split-off part of the self home into the wholeness of self in the hearth of our heart. This is an essential requirement to the process of our soul's identity shift from fallen human ground into spiritual redemption and inner resurrection. To accomplish it, we need help from the divine therapist.

On the other hand, repressing our dark shadow-side into the unconscious, rejecting and alienating it from our wholeness of self, is an act of cruelty toward our self. It is a manipulation of evil in our soul. That is, it's a cruel manifestation of hatred in that we are rejecting and separating our unhealed shadow-self. It's a manifestation of lies in that we are in conscious denial of the full truth of our self. And it's a manifestation of slavery in that rejecting and denying our shadow side, hating it and lying to our self about it, keeps it split-off from consciousness and perpetuates our bondage to its unhealthy subterranean expressions, e.g., egocentric selfishness, emotional happiness programs, afflictive emotions and perversions.

The only thing that could be worse than repressing the shadow-self into unconsciousness is the opposite extreme of psychotic, conscious over-identification with it. In this case, where our shadow-self dominates consciousness, we become possessed by our dark side and succumb to acting-out the worst, most dangerous tendencies of our cruel and perverse evil nature, i.e., sadomasochism and the creation of destruction. Until we are ready and willing to admit the full truth of our soul, as the grace of divine action reveals it to us, we are bound to remain stuck in status-quo cycles of our current separate-self identity and consciousness in human ground.

Fortunately, God is good and merciful. We simply need to humbly ask for help, consent to the divine action, trust and cooperate with the divine therapist as our dark hidden truths are revealed. In other words, grace does the healing and hard work of creating us anew, but we too have an essential role to play in this process, since it requires our conscious cooperation and willingness to see the truth and let go of all obstacles and attachments that hold us in bondage as unwitting captives. It requires repentance: that is, as Thomas Keating says, "changing the direction in which we're looking for happiness." If we do our part then God will do God's part and, as Jesus taught, "The truth will set us free" (John 8:32).

So our identity shift from false self to true self cannot happen without integrating our shadow-self and dark side, which amounts to making peace and friends with our inner enemy. Until we do so, we cannot have true peace of mind, freedom from inner fears and we cannot really know our self as we truly are. Our spiritual victory is to be won through love, peace and forgiveness, not through hatred, fear and violence. This is the meaning and fruit of manifesting love, truth and freedom in our soul and in our relationships with others. In doing so, we become the change that is needed in our world, and we become the message God longs to communicate to humanity through humanity. It is this that brings spiritual ground into human ground and the shifting of our identity from false self to true self.

VI

As mentioned earlier, intimacy is a lightning rod for storms in our soul's emotional energy-field. Love, the soul-force of intimacy, draws all things to itself and makes them new. Love's holy power transforms the shadow. In healing the wounded shadow-self, deep intimacy and love restore our lost innocence. This is what happens in us, in our intimate relationship with God, if we consent and allow it to happen. The divine therapist brings our frightening dark side into the light, our shadow-self into consciousness in order to heal it.

We instinctively recoil from this repressed material surfacing in our soul because we fear it, fear to be overwhelmed as it threatens the security and stability of our ego-strength and conscious, status-quo self-image. Love challenges us to trust the divine action when it reveals our dark side and unhealed wounds. It doesn't just reveal our unconscious contents as distant objects to be observed, but as living subjectivity to be experienced first-hand in the immediacy of our most intimate consciousness, one with us in the living now-moment and not separate. Such humbling experiences are high drama in the soul, real as anything we may feel that's alive in us.

Our unconscious contents and dark side may also be brought into waking consciousness via the mechanism of divine projection in close intimate relationships. Because of this, each deepening level of intimacy and vulnerability in a relationship, whether with another person, our self or with God, requires a correspondingly deeper level of openness and trust on our part. Caring intimacy and vulnerability open us to the beauty of love's preciousness. So the ultimate risk of separate-self security in relation to God or another offers the potential of an ultimate reward of separate-self transcendence and renewal in love's (Christ's) mystical body to enter in.

Again, love draws all things to itself, bringing up what needs to be revealed and healed, showing us hidden truths of our whole self. In doing so, the grace of love gives us opportunities to see our self as we really are, opportunities to let go of childish happiness programs, self-centered agendas and inner fears. Will we be able to recognize and trust in love's divine action when happiness programs are frustrated or gratified, and we lose the inner balance of our ego-strength and spiritual poise? The divine therapy can work for us only if we can work with it, giving it our willing consent, cooperation and trust.

## VII

Our true self transcends cultural conditioning. As we become increasingly identified with our deep inner self in spiritual ground, the contents of cultural conditioning become more and more secondary rather than a primary source of our identity sense. Of course, our culturally conditioned identity in human ground is an essential part of who we are as a human being in this world; but it's not who we ultimately are as a maturing child of non-created Reality (God).

There comes a point in our inner identity-shift process from false self to true self where we are able to consciously separate from our cultural conditioning, especially from its negative shadow aspects. When this happens, we gain the self-awareness, independence and inner freedom needed to consciously choose which aspects of cultural conditioning to embrace and which ones to reject. The criteria for choosing whether to accept or reject aspects of cultural conditioning come from the values of our innate conscience, and from how well we are served or not served by the ways in which these aspects of cultural conditioning influence us. Are they life-giving? Do they support our true self or our false self?

A new freedom arises in us as we awaken into awareness of our false self and our true self. This freedom allows us to become increasingly able to consciously choose and eventually control the programming of cultural conditioning in us, rather than having it control us. The same holds true for our conscious and unconscious emotional happiness programs which, as already mentioned, tend to interface with the negative, unhealthy aspects of cultural conditioning. It's important to remember that cultural conditioning, like the human beings who create it, has both healthy, life-affirming aspects and pathological dark aspects. Our practical challenge is to distinguish between these critical elements, in both our self and the world around us.

The goodness of our cultural conditioning needs to be honored and affirmed. It gives us so much of personal identity and our sense of place in human ground, as well as our sense of connection and common identity with others with whom we share its heritage. The cultural diversity and ethnic heritages of all human groups are to be honored and celebrated, at least in their positive, life-affirming aspects. Human cultural diversity is living testimony to the rich creativity, resourcefulness and beauty of the human spirit.

If we become over-identified and too wrapped up in cultural conditioning, we miss the greater identity of our deep inner self and intimate relationship with God, which connects us in loving oneness to all life, creation and consciousness. The intimacy/belonging we may experience via the group-mind of cultural conditioning cannot compare to the deep intimacy we may share with another person in intimate relationship or experience with the divine presence alive in our soul. The power of deep intimacy and love transforms who we are, drawing us into the great identity shift from our outer false self into our inner true self. As this happens, our outer self or personality becomes renewed and re-created in the living image and presence of the divine light in our soul. The passageway of this inner transformation in our soul is guarded by our innate conscience, and the way into it is through our growth in humility and love.

A key point of identity shift from human ground to spiritual ground involves putting our human identity into perspective with our spiritual identity. This is not an "either-or" proposition but an integrative one where our human identity becomes subsumed into our greater spiritual identity. We typically begin by having this relationship reversed; that is, we view our spiritual identity from the perspective of our human identity. This amounts to viewing our true self from the perspective of our false self, which is generally how we have to begin since we are living primarily in the consciousness of our false self, i.e., our separate-self sense and human personality. Identity shift involves a reversal of this initial relationship, a diminution of our false self in favor of our true self.

The Greek word "persona" means "mask" or "disguise." Like the clothes we wear on our body, our human personality or persona is the apparent identity we present to the world. This false self is a real self, a necessary and relatively real self, but it's not our permanent identity. It's more an instrument that we have and use for functioning in this world. Just as we may change the way we dress up our physical persona with grooming and clothing, so may we, with God's help, make changes in our personality to suit our better intentions and goals.

So the main identity shift in the human soul's evolution is from the mixed motivation of the false self into the pure motivation of the true self expressing the higher values, motivation and presence of spiritual ground. This, at least, is the ideal of spiritual identity shift. What it means in practical terms is that the outer personality becomes transformed and reborn into a harmonious expression of our innate spiritual nature or deep inner self. This is the ideal of human spiritual perfection represented and modeled for us by the great spiritual teachers of humanity, such at Gotama Buddha and Jesus Christ.

These extraordinary individuals, and several others, were human beings and divine beings at the same time manifested in the flesh, living in full consciousness of human ground and spiritual ground simultaneously. An important part of their message to us is that we all possess within us the same spiritual potential as manifested by their lives and consciousness. We are all invited to enter into communion and union with their spiritual awakening into the divine consciousness of non-created Reality or God, the Ultimate Mystery. This is the ultimate goal of identity shift from false self to true self and from human ground into spiritual ground.

Since most of us apparently do not fully experience the inner spiritual awakening and transformation of identity shift from human ground to spiritual ground during our human life, the question arises, "What about this? Does it mean we've failed or lost our opportunity?"

Answer: absolutely not. If, as Thomas Keating suggests, the false self drops away after physical death along with the physical body, then what are we to be left with? It seems we'll be left with our individual history and soul intact, minus the physical body and false self as our central point of reference and identity.

So, when the permanent identity shift from human ground to spiritual ground does not occur during our life in human ground, then most likely it will occur at some point in the next phase or phases of our existence—that is, somewhere in the higher, nonphysical spiritual ground, where our consciousness will reside following physical death. It may occur, for example, either during or following our soul's life-review process that recapitulates, from the loving perspective of our true self and conscience, all the details and relationships of our recently completed life in human ground. I suspect that our experience of this postmortem life-review process will depend not only on the specific events and relationships being reviewed, but on how and where our consciousness (sense of self) is or was identified as well. Be that as it may, physical death and its aftermath form a fascinating topic and obviously comprise one of the greatest mysteries of our spiritual life and relationship to God. We shall discover for certain the reality of what these mysteries actually are only when we undergo physical death and experience them for our self, first-hand.

# ENDNOTES

## Introduction

1. See Freud's *Complete Introductory Lectures on Psychanalysis,* Erikson's *Childhood and Society,* and Maslow's *Toward a Psychology of Being.* Also see appendix two: "Spiritual Genesis in Relation to Contemporary Developmental Psychology" in *The Spiritual Journey* by Francis Kelly Nemeck and Marie Theresa Coombs.

2. See Jung, *Man and His Symbols* and *Analytical Psychology,* as well as his autobiographical *Memories, Dreams, Reflections;* also Roberto Assagioli, *Psychosynthesis;* and Ken Wilber, *Sex, Ecology, Spirituality* and *Integral Spirituality.*

3. For information regarding Centering Prayer and its immediate conceptual background, see Thomas Keating's books *Open Mind, Open Heart; Invitation to Love; The Mystery of Christ; Intimacy with God; The Human Condition;* and *Manifesting God.*

4. Some of these sources are: *Bradshaw On: The Family: A New Way of Creating Solid Self-Esteem* by John Bradshaw; *Up from Eden* and *Sex, Ecology, and Spirituality* by Ken Wilber; *When Society Becomes an Addict* by Ann Wilson Schaef; *The Ego and the Dynamic Ground: A Transpersonal Theory of Human Development* by Michael Washburn; and *Christ and Consciousness* by William Thompson.

5. I first heard these words, "life-giving treasure," in reference to Thomas Keating's legacy spoken by Gail Fitzpatrick-Hopler at Contemplative Outreach's Twentieth Anniversary Meeting in Toronto, Ontario, in 2004.

6. Some indication of the wide range of interpretations of Genesis 1-3 is given as follows: In her interesting and informative book, *Adam, Eve and the Serpent,* biblical scholar Elaine Pagels describes some differing and conflicting interpretations of the fall held in ancient Jewish Tradition and by early Christians. For example, attitudes toward human sexuality in early Christianity, derived from Genesis 1–3, ranged from affirmation to negation. God's injunction to be fruitful and multiply (Genesis 1:28) combined with God saw everything that he had made, and indeed, it was very good (Genesis 1:31) may be seen to affirm sexual activity. On the other hand, Adam and Eve's apparent embarrassment and shame regarding their genitals after eating the "forbidden fruit," when they knew that they were naked (Genesis 2:7) combined with their expulsion from Paradise may be seen to call the goodness of human sexuality into question.
    According to Ms. Pagels, "By the beginning of the fifth century, Augustine had actually declared that spontaneous sexual desire is the proof of—and penalty for—universal original sin, an idea that would

have baffled most of his Christian predecessors, to say nothing of his pagan and Jewish contemporaries," p. xviii. Dr. Pagels points out that prior to St. Augustine, most Jewish and Christian interpreters of Genesis 1–3 rejected the idea that Adam's sin and the fall were due to sexual indulgence. Instead, Adam's sin that brought on the fall was believed to be disobedience. From this comes the more commonly accepted interpretation that disobedience and moral responsibility (human free will) form the real theme of the Adam and Eve story.

Elaine Pagels' research brought her to the conclusion that, "for nearly the first four hundred years of our era, Christians regarded freedom as the primary message of Genesis 1–3—freedom in its many forms.... With Augustine, this message was changed," p. xxv. St. Augustine—who struggled with personal sexual issues, as his *Confessions* clearly reveals—is perhaps the most influential theologian for Western Christianity. This same Augustine of Hippo, who has contributed so much of spiritual value and insight to Western Christianity, apparently projected his own exaggerated personal struggle with sexual lust and addiction into his interpretation of the Adam and Eve story—assuming that his main problem or temptation was also everyone else's. This complicated issue was perhaps his personal blind spot or Achilles Heel, and it has had tremendous negative impact on Western and Christian attitudes toward human sexuality ever since.

In his seminal early work, *Up From Eden: A Transpersonal View of Human Evolution*, integral philosopher Ken Wilbur puts forward the idea that rather than being kicked out of the Garden of Eden, Adam and Eve "got up and walked out." Another, more allegorical interpretation of the Adam and Eve myth comes from the mystical Qabalah, which has origins in the ancient Hebrew Tradition. According to this tradition, Adam represents generic humanity and Adam and Eve are not two separate beings but represent self-consciousness and sub-consciousness respectively in all of us, the fall being our emergence from the subtle World of Formation into physical incarnation in the World of Manifestation. This is explained by Rev. Ann Davies in a set of recorded lectures concerning Genesis 1–3. Akin to ancient Qabalistic interpretations, Elaine Pagels, in *Adam, Eve and the Serpent*, writes of some Christian Gnostics who, "read the story of Adam and Eve as an allegory of religious experience, as relating to the discovery of the authentic spiritual self (Eve) hidden within the soul (Adam)," p. xxiv.

## 1. Our Lost Paradise

1.  Altered states of consciousness involving experiential memories of orgasm and conception on the cellular level, though rare, have been reported. See, for example, "Winning the Sperm Race" in Stanislov Grof's fascinating memoir, *When the Impossible Happens: Adventures in Non-Ordinary Realities* (2006).

2.  Also see Robert A. Johnson's books, *She* and *He,* on feminine and masculine psychology.

3.  See J. E. Cirlot, *A Dictionary of Symbols;* Alexander Eliot, Mircea Eliade and Joseph Campbell, *Myths;* and Elaine Pagels, *Adam, Eve and the Serpent.*

4. In Matthew 10:16, Jesus says to his disciples, "See, I am sending you out like sheep into the midst of wolves; so be wise as serpents and innocent as doves."

5. See Jung's autobiographical *Memories, Dreams and Reflections* (p. 38).

## 2. Fruits of the Fall

1. The term *original sin* was coined by St. Augustine of Hippo (354–430CE).

2. This assumes the infant is born from what's come to be called a "good womb" as opposed to a "bad womb." See Stanislav Grof's discussions of Perinatal Matrices in his books, *Realms of the Human Unconscious* (pp. 95–115) and *Beyond the Brain* (pp. 98–127).

## 4. Good/Evil in Human Ground

1. Life's pure springing fountains represent the timeless primal orgasm of undifferentiated bliss at the initiation or beginning of creation and evolution, before the fall and the subsequent drama of creation begins. Life's pure springing fountains are the "Big Bang" of created reality's origins on the level of divine primal consciousness. They are the alpha or starting point of consciousness evolution's epic journey through time and creation. They are not the omega or final endpoint. The error of mistaking the primal bliss and undifferentiated unity of creation's origins with the ultimate spiritual awakening has been discussed by a number of accomplished spiritual teachers and writers. For example, see Sri Aurobindo, *The Synthesis of Yoga*; Lama Anagarika Govinda, *Creative Meditation and Multidimensional Consciousness*; and the Reverend Dr. Ann Davies's "Tree of Life" audio teaching series; her "Tarot" series; and "Genesis" in her lectures, set 3.

2. See *Invitation to Love*; *Intimacy with God*; *The Mystery of Christ*; *Open Mind, Open Heart*; and *Manifesting God*.

## 5. Our Basic Needs: Part One

1. Guy Murchie's monumental work, *The Seven Mysteries of Life*, details the evolution of matter, life and consciousness in the physical Universe. Also see Pierre Tielhard De Chardin, *Man's Place in Nature* and Lynne McTaggart, *The Field*.

2. I first encountered this concept in a privately published article, "The Significance of Meditation in Buddhism," by Lama Anagarika Govinda in 1970.

3. Hear Robert A. Johnson's audio program, "The Golden World," published by Sounds True.

4. This teaching of the Buddha is recounted in Power, *The Lost Teachings of Lama Govinda*.

## 6. Our Basic Needs: Part Two

1. The "inner room," also translated as "closet" or "private room," is mentioned by Jesus in Matthew 6:6 where he teaches about prayer. Also see *Open Mind, Open Heart* by Thomas Keating for more on the "inner room."

## 7. Our Basic Needs: Part Three

1. These wise words are from Fr. Bernie Owens, S.J., at a silent contemplative retreat, "Discovering our Inner Depths," October, 2010, at Holy Spirit Center near Anchorage, Alaska.

2. Read "On Work," in *The Prophet*, by Kahlil Gibran.

## 8. False Self and Happiness Programs: Part One

1. T. Keating, *The Mystery of Christ*, p. 39.

2. The case for the unconscious food/love connection and its overcoming is made by Geneen Roth in the audio CD program, "When Food is Food and Love is Love" from Sounds True.

3. This unconscious search for transcendence is pointed out in Gerald May's insightful book, *Addiction and Grace*.

## 9. False Self and Happiness Programs: Part Two

1. I heard this expression, "domination has no place in love," from Swami Amar Jyoti at a spiritual retreat in the 1970s.

2. In his book, *The Biology of Belief*, and his audio program, "The Wisdom of Your Cells," biologist Bruce Lipton explains how cooperation rather than competition is the real basis of progressive evolution in terrestrial life forms. Also see psychologist Alfie Kohn's informative book, *No Contest: The Case Against Competition—Why We Lose in Our Race to Win*.

## 10. Intimacy/Belonging and Happiness Programs

1. See, for example, Keating's books, *Open Mind, Open Heart; Invitation to Love; Intimacy with God;* and *Manifesting God*.

2. I found the "lightning rod" metaphor in Harriet Lerner, *The Dance of Intimacy*, p. 48.

## 11. *Identity Quest and Cultural Conditioning*

1.  A vivid, poignant example of the human slave trade in South America is portrayed in the 1986 film, *The Mission,* based on a true story and available on DVD (Warner Bros.).

## 12. *Cultural Conditioning and Identity Shift*

1.  See Carl Jung, *Man and his Symbols,* and Collected Works, vol. 9, part 1, *The Archetypes and the Collective Unconscious,* and vol. 9, part 2, *Aion: Researches Into the Phenomenology of the Self.* William A. Miller's book, *Make Friends with Your Shadow,* is a very readable, Christian-based treatment of this subject.

2.  Unconditional forgiveness of others is a fundamental part of the revolutionary spiritual teaching introduced and modeled by Jesus in the gospels. For example, when Peter asked Jesus, "Lord, if another member of the church sins against me, how often should I forgive? As many as seven times?" Jesus said to him, "Not seven times, but, I tell you, seventy-seven times," Matthew 18:21–22. When he was crucified and in the throes of death, Jesus prayed, "Father, forgive them; for they do not know what they are doing," Luke 23:34. In teaching the famous Lord's Prayer, Jesus enjoins us to pray, "And forgive us our debts as we also have forgiven our debtors," Matthew 6:12. The role of forgiveness in living Christ's gospel is a natural expression of the primacy of love for all in Jesus' teaching and example. A good book on this subject is *The Process of Forgiveness* by Fr. William A. Meninger. Also hear "The Beginner's Guide to Forgiveness" by Buddhist meditation teacher, Jack Kornfield, available from Sounds True.

# References

Assagioli, R. *Psychosynthesis*. New York: Viking, 1965.

Aurobindo, Sri. *The Synthesis of Yoga*. Pondicherry, India: Sri Aurobindo Ashram, 1955.

Bradshaw, J. *Bradshaw On: The Family: A New Way of Creating Solid Self-Esteem*. Deerfield Beach, FL: Health Communications, 1988.

Cirlot, J. E. *A Dictionary of Symbols*. New York: Philosophical Library, 1962.

de Chardin, P. T. *Man's Place in Nature*. New York: Harper & Row, 1966.

Eliot, A., M. Eliade, and J. Campbell. *The Universal Myths: Heroes, Gods, Tricksters, and Others*. New York: McGraw-Hill, 1976.

Erikson, E. H. *Childhood and Society*. New York: Norton, 1963.

Freud, S. *The Complete Introductory Lectures on Psychoanalysis*. New York: Norton, 1962.

Gibran, K. *The Prophet*. New York: Alfred P. Knopf, 1923.

Govinda, Lama Anagarika. *Creative Meditation and Multidimensional Consciousness*. Wheaton, IL: Theosophical Publishing House, 1976.

Grof, S. *Beyond the Brain: Birth, Death, and Transcendence in Psychotherapy*. Albany: SUNY, 1985.

———. *Realms of the Human Unconsciousness: Observations from LSD Research*. New York: Dutton, 1976.

———. *When the Impossible Happens: Adventures in Non-Ordinary Reality*. Boulder, CO: Sounds True, 2006.

*Holy Bible: New Revised Standard Version*. New York: Oxford University Press, 1989.

Johnson, R. *He: Understanding Masculine Psychology*. New York: Harper & Row, 1989.

———. *She: Understanding Feminine Psychology*. New York: Harper & Row, 1989.

———. *We: Understanding the Psychology of Romantic Love*. San Francisco: Harper, 1983.

Jung, C. G. *The Colleced Works of C. G. Jung*. Princeton: Bollingen Series XX, Princeton Univ. Press:

———. *Aion: Researches into the Phenomenology of the Self*, vol. 9, Part 2.

———. *Analytical Psychology*. New York: Vintage, 1968.

———. *The Archetypes and the Collective Unconscious*, vol. 9, Part 1, 1980.

———, et al. *Man and his Symbols*. New York: Doubleday, 1964.

———. *Memories, Dreams, Reflections*. New York: Vintage, 1965.

Keating, T. *Open Mind, Open Heart: The Contemplative Dimension of the Gospel*, 20th Anniversary Edition. New York: Continuum, 2006.

———. *Invitation to Love: The Way of Christian Contemplation*. New York: Continuum, 1992.

———. *The Mystery of Christ: The Liturgy as Spiritual Experience*. New York: Continuum, 2003.

———. *The Human Condition: Contemplation and Transformation*. New York: Paulist, 1999.

———. *Intimacy with God: An Introduction to Centering Prayer*. New York: Crossroad, 1994.

———. *Manifesting God*. New York: Lantern Books, 2005.

Kohn, A. *No Contest: The Case Against Competition*. Boston: Houghton Mifflin, 1986.

Lerner, H. *The Dance of Intimacy: A Woman's Guide to Courageous acts of Change in Key Relationships*. New York: Harper Perennial,1989.

Lipton, B. H. *The Biology of Belief: Unleashing the Power of Consciousness, Matter, & Miracles*. Santa Rosa, CA: Mountain of Love/Elite Books, 2005.

Maslow, A. *Toward a Psychology of Being*. New York: Van Nostrand Reinhold, 1968.

May, G. G. *Addiction and Grace: Love and Spirituality in the Healing of Addictions*. San Francisco: Harper, 1991.

McTaggart, Lynne. *The Field: The Quest for the Secret Force of the Universe*. New York: Harper, 2008.

Meninger, W. A. *The Process of Forgiveness*. New York: Continuum, 1996.

Miller, W. A. *Make Friends with Your Shadow: How to Accept and Use Positively the Negative Side of Your Personality*. Minneapolis: Augsburg, 1981.

Murchie, G. *The Seven Mysteries of Life: An Exploration of Science and Philosophy*. Boston: Houghton Mifflin, 1981.

Nemeck, F. K. and M.T. Coombs. *The Spiritual Journey: Critical Thresholds and Stages of Adult Spiritual Genesis*. Collegeville, MN: Liturgical Press, 1987.

Pagels, E. *Adam, Eve and the Serpent*. New York: Vintage, 1988.

Power, R., ed. *The Lost Teachings of Lama Govinda: Living Wisdom from a Modern Tibetan Master*. Wheaton, IL: Theosophical Publishing House, 2007.

Schaef, A. W. *When Society Becomes an Addict*. New York: Harper & Row, 1987.

Thompson, W. M. *Christ and Consciousness: Exploring Christ's Contribution to Human Consciousness*. New York: Paulist Press, 1977.

Washburn, M. *The Ego and the Dynamic Ground*. Albany: SUNY, 1988.

Wilber, K. *Integral Spirituality: A Startling New Role for Religion in the Modern and Postmodern World*. Boston: Integral Books, 2006.

———. *Sex, Ecology, Spirituality: The Spirit of Evolution*. Boston: Shambhalah, 2002.

———. *Up from Eden: A Transpersonal View of Human Evolution*. Garden City, NY: Anchor/Doubleday, 1981.

## OTHER REFERENCES

### *Audio:*

Davies, A. *Lectures on Genesis 1–3 as understood in Qabalah*, Lecture Set 3, "Tree of Life" and "Tarot" CD Series. Available through Builders of the Adytum; ph.: 323-255-7141; or online: www.bota.org.

Johnson, R.A. *The Golden World: Our Search for Meaning, Fulfillment and Divine Beauty*. Available through Sounds True.

Kornfield, J. *The Beginner's Guide to Forgiveness*. Available from Sounds True.

Lipton, B. H. *The Wisdom of Your Cells: How Beliefs Control Your Biology*. Available from Sounds True; ph.: 800-333-9185; or online: www.soundstrue.com.

Roth, G. *When Food is Food and Love is Love*. Available from Sounds True.

### *Video:*

*The Mission*. Warner Bros., 1986.

**CONTEMPLATIVE OUTREACH** is a spiritual network of individuals and small faith communities committed to living the contemplative dimension of the Gospel. The common desire for Divine transformation, primarily expressed through a commitment to a daily Centering Prayer practice, unites our international, interdenominational community.

Today, Contemplative Outreach annually serves over 40,000 people; supports over 120 active contemplative chapters in 39 countries; supports over 800 prayer groups; teaches over 15,000 people the practice of Centering Prayer and other contemplative practices through locally-hosted workshops; and provides training and resources to local chapters and volunteers. We also publish and distribute the wisdom teachings of Fr. Thomas Keating and other resources that support the contemplative life.

*Contemplative Outreach, Ltd.*
*10 Park Place, 2nd Floor, Suite B*
*Butler, New Jersey 07405*

*973-838-3384*
*Fax 973-492-5795*
*Email: office@coutreach.org*
*www.contemplativeoutreach.org*

**KESS FREY** was born in 1945 and grew up in the Eagle Rock neighborhood of North Los Angeles. In 1968 he took a bachelor's degree in psychology at the University of California, Irvine. Since 1965, he has studied Eastern and Western philosophy, psychology and religion, with a background in meditation and depth psychology. He was raised Catholic and is a Catholic Christian who honors the contemplative dimension of all religions and spiritual paths. His principal spiritual teachers have been Lama Anagarika Govinda (German), Chogyam Trungpa, Rinpoche (Tibetan), Swami Amar Jyoti (East Indian), and, since 1989, Fr. Thomas Keating (American).

Mr. Frey has lived in Anchorage, Alaska since 1983, where he worked with school-age children for twenty years. He's been involved with Centering Prayer since 1989, is affiliated with Contemplative Outreach and offers introductory Centering Prayer workshops, facilitates prayer groups and silent retreats, and is active in prison ministry. He is also the author of two previous books, *Satsang Notes of Swami Amar Jyoti* and *The Creation of Reality*.